COOKIE COOKERY

COOKIE COOKERY

BY

JOHN J. ZENKER

AND

HAZEL G. ZENKER

M. EVANS AND COMPANY, INC.
New York, New York 10017

M. Evans and Company titles are distributed in
the United States by the J. B. Lippincott Company,
East Washington Square, Philadelphia, Pa. 19105;
and in Canada by McClelland & Stewart Ltd.,
25 Hollinger Road, Toronto M4B 3G2, Ontario

Library of Congress Catalog Card Number 69-18832

ISBN 0-87131-261-1 (Paperback)
ISBN 0-87131-041-4 (Hardcover)

Manufactured in the United States of America

9 8 7 6 5 4 3 2 1

*This book of the world's best cookies
is dedicated with respect and gratitude
to American homemakers and home economists
who do so much for the well-being and
good disposition of the opposite sex and
for the children of today and those to come*

KEEP THE COOKIE JAR FULL

ALMOST EVERYONE likes cookies, but perhaps youngsters are the biggest cookie fans. If there are children in your home there should be a cookie jar. Never empty. Freshly filled with their favorites for school lunch boxes, after-school snacks, picnics, parties, and handouts to their friends.

And a full cookie jar is an asset when your own friends drop in: a thin, delectable cookie is just right with tea or coffee. And an unusual cookie—one made with mysterious, or at least unknown ingredients—is the ideal light dessert at a bridge party or club tea. And much appreciated as the added charmer on the dinner ice cream dish or fruit parfait.

The recipes in this book include traditional cookies known to most home cooks who like to bake. In addition, we have included rare, and special chef recipes, famous cookies from great hotels and pastry shops in Europe. Many are unusual cookies known only to foreign-trained chefs and to the skilled cooks in fine European homes.

Drop cookies, rolled cookies, pressed, cut, decorated cookies. Simple, luxurious, familiar, some strangely different, all delicious. These hundreds of good cookies provide you with a complete cookie cook book. An endless supply of the best, the most popular, the most unusual cookies to keep the cookie jar filled.

H. G. Z.

CONTENTS

FILLINGS, ICINGS AND FROSTINGS

COOKIE HELPERS

You MAY want to add to your kitchen some of the utensils and accessories which professional pastry cooks find helpful in making cookies.

Cookie cutters. There are many kinds available in five-and-ten cent stores and wherever kitchen wares are sold. Large, small, round, oblong, square, crescent, diamond, tree, star, flowers, animals, wreath and other shapes. Two-inch, two-and-one-half-inch, and three-inch round cutters are called for in some of these recipes, also very small cutters and a two-inch fluted cutter, a doughnut cutter, and a Christmas tree cookie cutter.

Cookie molds and presses. Small fancy-shape miniature pans for various rich cookies, a cookie press for many delicious European-type cookies, large and small molds of Santa Claus, gingerbread men, and various other American and imported shapes for holiday and other cookies.

Cookie Sheets. Two or more cookie sheets, and pans of different sizes, should be bright and shining for best results in baking. Some pans needed in various recipes: 8-inch square, 9-inch square, 10-by-15-inch with 1-inch rim (or sides), 11-by-17-inch pan, 12-by-8-inch shallow pan, 13-by-9-by-2-inch pan, and a 15-by-11-inch jelly roll pan.

Use baking sheets and pans small enough that there is at least one inch of heat circulation around the pan between it and the walls of your oven, otherwise cookies brown too quickly on the bottom. If pans with sides (instead of cookie sheets) are used, turn the pans upside down and bake cookies on the bottom of the pan. And always have *waxed paper and aluminum foil* with which to line a pan if the recipe says so.

Cooling racks. Let cookies cool on racks. Never pile hot cookies on top of each other to cool. Store cooled cookies in a jar with a tightly-fitting cover, or in a canister or tin box with snug cover.

Mixing bowls, flour sifter, pastry blender, standard measuring cup and set of standard measuring spoons, large kitchen spoons for mixing batter, egg beater, wire whip, pastry brush, large rubber plate-scraper with flexible points to remove dough from bowl (prevents waste and insures accuracy.) A candy thermometer for icings.

Pastry bag with large and small tube attachments for ladyfingers, cat's tongues and many other "squeezed" dough cookies, and for decorating cookies.

Pastry board. Or roll dough out on pastry cloth.

Pastry cloth and rolling-pin stocking are helpful in making rolled-dough cookies.

Spatulas are helpful in lifting unbaked cookies onto pans and removing hot cookies onto the cooling racks.

Springerle rolling pin rolls various designs right onto the dough before cutting and baking. Springerle boards are also available in import shops.

Follow Recipe Directions

Read the entire recipe before you begin to assemble the ingredients and utensils called for. If recipe includes melted chocolate, begin by placing the chocolate over hot water. If oven is to be preheated, start it, or if recipe is long and complicated, turn oven on when almost ready to finish mixing or to roll dough out.

If using an electric range follow the range's directions for the oven. Usually for cookies, after the electric oven registers the correct heat (according to the recipe) turn off the oven-top element and bake with it off.

If the dough recipe contains a large amount of shortening (fat, butter, cream) or if you are going to use a cookie press with it, do not grease the cookie sheets or pans. Follow the recipe instructions for baking.

For cookie bars, unless otherwise directed in the recipe, grease the cookie sheets and cover each with waxed paper, then grease the waxed paper. Place dough on the paper.

Or cookie-bar dough is baked in a square or oblong pan, and when done cut into squares or oblongs.

For macaroons and meringues, cover baking sheets with two layers of paper toweling or with heavy brown paper. Or follow recipe directions.

Refrigerator dough is pressed into a cookie mold, or shaped into a thick bar or roll, chilled until ready to be cut into thin slices, then baked according to recipe instructions.

Cookies burn easily especially those made with molasses and no milk. Watch them, turn the pans around frequently while baking to insure even browning.

After each pan of cookies is baked, wipe the pan or cookie sheet with heavy paper toweling slightly greased. Let cool before baking the next batch. Never put cookies on a hot pan. If a large batch is to be made use several pans or cookie sheets, so there is at least one cold pan for each batch.

To estimate the number of cookies in a recipe, if you decide to use different cutter than the one called for: a mixture containing 1½-cups flour makes 24 small (1½-inch) cookies, or other small shapes.

COOKIE COOKERY

1. ALMOND COOKIES

FRENCH ALMOND CRESCENTS

INGREDIENTS	METHOD
1 cup (purchased) almond paste ¾ cup confectioners' sugar 1 egg white	*Mix slowly with wooden spoon until well blended.*
¾ cup confectioners' sugar 2 egg whites	*Add sugar and remaining 2 egg whites and blend well.*

SPECIAL INSTRUCTIONS: Put mixture in pastry bag with No. 3 star tube and squeeze out crescents and different shapes onto cookie pans covered with heavy brown paper. Bake.

Oven Temperature: 325 degrees Fahrenheit.

Baking Time: 18 to 20 minutes.

After baking and while still hot, brush with Simple Syrup (Page 304). Turn upside-down, wet paper with damp cloth and remove crescents. Leave plain, decorate with candied fruit, or cover with Bittersweet Chocolate Coating (Page 291).

Makes about 4 dozen crescents.

ALMOND COOKIES

INGREDIENTS	METHOD
½ cup butter 1 cup granulated sugar	*Cream together.*
1 egg	*Add and mix well.*
½ cup milk 1 tsp. grated lemon rind	*Add and blend.*
2¾ cups all-purpose flour ½ tsp. salt 1½ tsps. baking powder	*Sift flour with salt and baking powder, fold in and mix.*
1 can almond filling	*See method for topping cookies suggested below.*

SPECIAL INSTRUCTIONS: Roll dough thin, cut in various shapes. Top cookies with almond filling. Bake.

Oven Temperature: 400 degrees Fahrenheit.

Baking Time: 10 to 12 minutes.

NOTE: To top the cookies with almond filling, use canvas or paper pastry bag. Use small opening or tube and squeeze small amount of filling onto each cookie. (Prepared almond filling is available in most large food stores and in bakery supply shops.)

Makes about 4 dozen.

BROWN ALMOND DROP COOKIES

INGREDIENTS	METHOD
½ cup butter or margarine 3 oz. (squares) unsweetened chocolate	*Melt together over low heat. Do not let boil. Remove from heat.*
1½ cups granulated sugar	*Stir in.*
3 eggs	*Add 1 at a time, beat well after each addition.*
1½ cups all-purpose flour 1 cup chopped toasted almonds *	*Blend in flour and nuts.*

SPECIAL INSTRUCTIONS: Drop by rounded teaspoon onto greased cookie pans. Bake.

Oven Temperature: 350 degrees Fahrenheit.

Baking Time: 12 to 15 minutes.

NOTE: When salted butter is used, no salt is needed in this recipe. However, when using margarine add a pinch of salt to the mixture.

* Other nuts, such as pecans and walnuts, may be used in place of almonds and can be bought already chopped.

Makes 2 to 3 dozen drop cookies.

ORIENTAL ALMOND COOKIES

INGREDIENTS	METHOD
1 cup butter 1 cup granulated sugar	*Cream together until blended.*
1 egg 1 tsp. almond extract	*Add and mix well.*
1¾ cups all-purpose flour ½ tsp. baking powder	*Sift together and combine with the above mixture.*
Milk **Whole blanched almonds**	*See instructions below.*

SPECIAL INSTRUCTIONS: Roll dough ¼ inch thick on floured cloth or board and cut with a 2-inch round cookie cutter. Place cookies on lightly greased cookie pan. Brush lightly with milk and press a whole almond in center of each cookie. Bake.

Oven Temperature: 350 to 375 degrees Fahrenheit.

Baking Time: about 10 to 12 minutes or until lightly browned.

Makes about 2 dozen cookies.

2. BARS, FINGERS, SQUARES AND STICKS

ALMOND BARS

INGREDIENTS	METHOD
½ cup margarine ⅛ tsp. salt 1 cup granulated sugar	*Cream together until fluffy.*
1 cup all-purpose flour	*Sift.*
1 tsp. almond extract 1¾ cups grated almonds	*Add with the flour to sugar mixture and mix thoroughly.*

SPECIAL INSTRUCTIONS: Roll out dough on a floured cloth to about ¼-inch thickness. Cut into bars about 2 inches long and ½ inch wide. Place in lightly greased cookie pans. Bake.

Oven Temperature: 350 degrees Fahrenheit.

Baking Time: about 18 to 20 minutes.

When cool, dip bars in confectioners' sugar.

Makes about 1½ dozen bars.

PLAIN BAR COOKIES

INGREDIENTS	METHOD
¾ cup margarine	*Cream.*
½ cup granulated sugar	*Add gradually, creaming until light.*
2 eggs	*Add 1 at a time, mix thoroughly after each addition.*
1½ cups all-purpose flour 1 tsp. baking powder ¼ tsp. salt	*Sift flour with baking powder and salt.*
¼ cup milk 1 tsp. vanilla	*Combine, add alternately with flour mixture to the sugar-egg mixture. Blend smoothly.*

SPECIAL INSTRUCTIONS: Spread evenly in well greased and floured 12 by 9 by 2-inch pan. Bake.

Oven Temperature: 350 degrees Fahrenheit.

Baking Time: 20 to 25 minutes.

Let cool in pan. When cool spread with strawberry jam and pour Lemon Confectioners' Sugar Icing in thin streams over the top (Page 302). Or frost with Chocolate Frosting (Page 294). Cut in bars.

Makes 18 2 by 3-inch bars.

CHOCOLATE BAR COOKIES

INGREDIENTS	METHOD
1 cup shortening	*Cream for about 3 minutes.*
2 cups brown sugar 4 eggs	*Add sugar and eggs alternately and beat well.*
½ tsp. salt 2 tsps. vanilla 4 oz. (squares) unsweetened chocolate	*Melt chocolate over hot water, blend into egg mixture with salt and vanilla.*
1 cup all-purpose flour ¼ tsp. baking powder	*Sift flour and baking powder together and add to creamed mixture.*
1½ cups finely chopped walnuts	*Blend in.*

SPECIAL INSTRUCTIONS: Pour into 2 8 by 8 by 2-inch lightly greased and floured pans. Bake.
Oven Temperature: 325 degrees Fahrenheit.
Baking Time: 30 to 35 minutes.
Let cool slightly in pans. Cut into squares or oblongs.
Makes about 30 bars.

CAKE-CRUMB BARS

INGREDIENTS	METHOD
2 cups shortening 4 cups brown sugar	*Cream together.*
4 eggs, beaten	*Stir in until smooth.*
3 cups seedless raisins ½ cup finely chopped nuts 1 tblsp. vanilla	*Wash and drain raisins. Add with nuts and vanilla.*
1 tblsp. baking soda 2½ cups cream, milk or sour milk	*Mix soda with milk.*
4½ cups all-purpose flour ½ cup soya-bean flour 3 cups cake crumbs° 1 tblsp. salt 1½ tblsps. powdered cinnamon	*Sift together flours, salt and cinnamon. Add alternately with crumbs and milk-and-soda solution to the sugar-egg-and-nut mixture.*
2 cups uncooked oatmeal	*Add to flour mixture and stir until blended.*

° The cake crumbs are the crumblings of left-over cakes or a few day-old cookies. Dry these on a baking pan in a warm oven, roll into crumbs and store in tightly covered jars until needed.

SPECIAL INSTRUCTIONS: Spoon mixture into large, greased cookie pans. Bake.

Oven Temperature: 350 degrees Fahrenheit.

Baking Time: 15 to 20 minutes.

Before cutting, ice with Cream Icing (Page 300). When icing has set, cut in squares or bars.

This large-quantity recipe makes 96 or more bars depending on size. Ideal for church suppers, cake sales and similar occasions.

CHOCOLATE NUT SQUARES

INGREDIENTS	METHOD
1 cup butter or margarine 1 cup brown sugar 1 egg yolk 1 tsp. vanilla	*Cream together.*
2 cups all-purpose flour ¼ tsp. salt	*Sift flour with salt. Stir into butter mixture until blended.*
4 or 5 oz. (squares) chocolate, from thin milk-chocolate bars ¾ cup chopped walnuts	*See instructions below.*

SPECIAL INSTRUCTIONS: Pat dough into a rectangle, 12½ by 10½ inches, on a greased cookie pan, leaving 1 inch around edge of cookie pan. Bake.

Oven Temperature: 350 degrees Fahrenheit.

Baking Time: 20 to 25 minutes until nicely browned. The baked dough will be soft.

Remove from oven. Immediately place separated squares of chocolate on top. Let stand until chocolate is soft. Spread evenly over surface and sprinkle with nuts. Cut into small squares while still warm.

Makes about 80 small squares.

BROWN-SUGAR BARS

INGREDIENTS	METHOD
1 cup margarine 1 cup brown sugar 1 tsp. almond extract	*Cream together.*
2 cups all-purpose flour	*Sift and add to above. Mix.*
6 oz. (squares) bittersweet chocolate	*Melt over hot water.*
1 cup chopped pecans	*Add to flour mixture together with the melted chocolate.*

SPECIAL INSTRUCTIONS: Mix thoroughly. Pour into a 10 by 15 by 1-inch cookie pan and spread evenly. Bake.

Oven Temperature: 350 degrees Fahrenheit.

Baking Time: 20 to 25 minutes.

Let cool slightly, then cut in 2 by 1-inch bars. Dust with confectioners' sugar.

Makes 75 bars.

Chocolate Nut Squares

CHOCOLATE PEANUT BARS

INGREDIENTS	METHOD
⅓ cup butter	*Melt in top of double boiler. Remove from heat.*
1 cup brown sugar	*Blend in. Let cool slightly.*
1 tsp. vanilla 2 eggs	*Add vanilla. Blend in eggs 1 at a time, beating well after each.*
1⅓ cups all-purpose flour 1 tsp. baking powder ½ tsp. salt	*Sift together flour, baking powder and salt, add to egg mixture. Blend well.*

SPECIAL INSTRUCTIONS: Spread into a well greased 9 by 9 by 2-inch pan. Bake.

Oven Temperature: 375 degrees Fahrenheit.

Baking Time: 15 to 18 minutes.

Let cool slightly. Spread lightly with Peanut-Butter Topping, then carefully spread with the Chocolate Topping. If desired sprinkle ¼ cup peanuts, chopped fine, over the chocolate. When cold, cut in bars.

Makes about 21 bars.

PEANUT-BUTTER TOPPING

INGREDIENTS	METHOD
½ cup peanut butter 1 tblsp. cream	*Heat in top of double boiler over hot water, stirring to blend well. Do not boil. Remove from hot water.*

CHOCOLATE TOPPING	
INGREDIENTS	METHOD
1 cup semi-sweet chocolate bits 1 tblsp. shortening	*Melt chocolate pieces over hot water, add shortening and blend well. Do not boil. Remove from hot water.*

CHOCOLATE-CHIP BARS

INGREDIENTS	METHOD
⅔ cup margarine 1 cup brown sugar 1 egg 1 tsp. vanilla	*Cream together thoroughly.*
1½ cups all-purpose flour ½ tsp. baking soda ½ tsp. salt	*Sift dry ingredients together, add to above and mix well.*
½ cup chopped nuts 6 oz. (tblsps.) chocolate bits	*Combine with flour mixture.*

SPECIAL INSTRUCTIONS: Spread batter in a greased oblong 13 by 9 by 2-inch pan. Bake.

Oven Temperature: 370 degrees Fahrenheit.

Baking Time: 25 minutes.

Let cool slightly in pan. Cut into bars.

Makes about 24 large bars.

GRANDMA'S BARS

INGREDIENTS	METHOD
5 eggs	*Beat in bowl.*
2 cups brown sugar	*Add to eggs and mix thoroughly.*
3 cups all-purpose flour 1 tsp. powdered cinnamon ½ tsp. ground cloves 2 tsps. baking powder 1 tsp. salt	*Sift together and add.*
1 package (7½ oz.) pitted dates, finely cut ½ cup pecan pieces 2 cups fruit-cake fruit 1 cup seedless raisins, washed and drained ½ cup dried apricots, if desired, cut fine	*Add to above and mix well.*

SPECIAL INSTRUCTIONS: Spread all the dough onto a 10 by 15-inch greased cookie pan. Bake.

Oven Temperature: 350 degrees Fahrenheit.

Baking Time: 30 minutes.

While still hot frost with Rum Icing (Page 300). When cool, cut in squares, diamonds or bars.

Makes 25 (2 by 3-inch) bars, or 50 or more diamonds or squares.

COCONUT-CRUNCH BARS

BOTTOM LAYER

INGREDIENTS	METHOD
1 cup all-purpose flour ⅓ cup brown sugar	*Sift together until blended.*
¼ cup shortening	*Cut into flour until mixture is in small crumbs.*

SPECIAL INSTRUCTIONS: Pat firmly into an 8-inch square pan. Bake.

Oven Temperature: 350 degrees Fahrenheit.

Baking Time: 12 minutes.

TOP LAYER

INGREDIENTS	METHOD
2 eggs	*Beat until light.*
1¼ cups brown sugar	*Add gradually, beat well.*
¼ cup all-purpose flour ½ tsp. vanilla 2 cups finely chopped or shredded coconut	*Fold in.*

SPECIAL INSTRUCTIONS: Spread on top of warm baked bottom layer. Return pan to oven. Bake.

Oven Temperature: 350 degrees Fahrenheit.

Baking Time: 20 to 25 minutes.

Cut into bars while warm.

Makes 32 narrow bars.

COCONUT SQUARES

BOTTOM

INGREDIENTS	METHOD
⅓ cup confectioners' sugar ⅓ cup margarine	*Cream together until light.*
½ tsp. vanilla ¼ tsp. almond extract 1 egg yolk	*Add and mix well.*
1 cup all-purpose flour	*Sift. Gradually mix into egg combination.*

SPECIAL INSTRUCTIONS: Press dough into a greased 9 by 9 by 2-inch pan. Bake.

Oven Temperature: 400 degrees Fahrenheit.

Baking Time: 9 minutes.

Remove from oven. Reduce oven heat to 350 degrees Fahrenheit.

TOP

INGREDIENTS	METHOD
½ cup light brown sugar 1 tblsp. all-purpose flour ½ tsp. baking powder ½ tsp. salt	*Mix all together.*
2 eggs	*Beat in.*

½ cup light corn syrup ½ cup finely chopped or shredded coconut 1 cup chopped pecans ½ tsp. vanilla	*Add, blend well.*

SPECIAL INSTRUCTIONS: Spread mixture over half-baked crust. Bake.

Oven Temperature: 350 degrees Fahrenheit.

Baking Time: 15 to 20 minutes, or until done.

Let cool and cut into squares.

Makes 16 or more squares.

DATE BARS

INGREDIENTS	METHOD
4 eggs 1 cup light brown sugar	*Beat together until thick.*
1¼ cups pitted, cut-up dates 1 cup chopped pecans	*Add to above.*
1 cup all-purpose flour 1 tsp. baking powder	*Sift and add to above, mixing until well blended.*

SPECIAL INSTRUCTIONS: Pour into a 9-inch square pan lined with waxed paper. Bake.

Oven Temperature: 325 degrees Fahrenheit.

Baking Time: 15 to 20 minutes, or until done.

When done, let cool. Remove paper. Cut into 2¼-inch bars.

NOTE: One 7½-ounce package pitted dates is 1¼ cups.

Makes 16 bars.

COCOA BARS

INGREDIENTS	METHOD
⅓ cup margarine	*Melt in saucepan. Remove from heat.*
¾ cup sugar	*Add and mix well.*
2 eggs ½ tsp. vanilla	*Blend in and mix thoroughly.*
⅔ cup all-purpose flour ¾ cup cocoa powder ½ tsp. baking powder	*Sift flour, cocoa and baking powder together and blend into egg mixture.*
1 cup pitted, finely cut dates ¾ cup finely chopped walnuts	*Stir in and mix well.*

SPECIAL INSTRUCTIONS: Spread in a well greased 9 by 9 by 2-inch pan. Sprinkle with chopped nuts. Bake.

Oven Temperature: 370 degrees Fahrenheit.

Baking Time: 25 minutes.

Let cool slightly, then cut into bars.

Makes about 18 bars.

DATE-NUT FINGERS

INGREDIENTS	METHOD
1 cup fine, granulated sugar 3 eggs	*Mix together, beat well.*
½ tsp. grated lemon rind ½ tsp. almond extract ½ tsp. salt	*Add to above and blend.*
¾ cup all-purpose flour 1 tsp. baking powder	*Sift together.*
½ cup finely chopped pecans ½ cup finely chopped pitted dates	*Add with flour to sugar mixture and blend thoroughly.*

SPECIAL INSTRUCTIONS: Pour into an 8-inch square pan greased or lined with paper which has been greased. Bake.
Oven Temperature: 350 degrees Fahrenheit.
Baking Time: 25 to 30 minutes.
Before completely cold cut in long fingers and cover with confectioners' sugar.

Makes 32 fingers.

DATE SQUARES

INGREDIENTS	METHOD
2 cups very finely cut pitted dates 1 lemon 1 orange	*Add grated peel and juice of lemon and orange to dates and let stand 12 hours, or overnight.*
4 eggs	*Beat until light.*
2 cups brown sugar	*Add to eggs with sifted ingredients.*
2 cups all-purpose flour ¼ tsp. salt 1 tsp. instant coffee powder 2 tsps. baking powder 2 tsps. powdered cinnamon	*Sift together.*
1 cup finely chopped nut meats	*Add with date mixture and blend well.*

SPECIAL INSTRUCTIONS: Spread ¼ inch thick in greased and floured 12 by 15-inch pan. Bake.

Oven Temperature: 375 degrees Fahrenheit.

Baking Time: 30 minutes

Let cool in pan. Spread with Orange Frosting (Page 304). Cut in 1½-inch squares.

Makes 80 squares.

FLORIDA ALMOND BARS

INGREDIENTS	METHOD
2 cups all-purpose flour ⅓ cup granulated sugar 1½ tsps. baking powder ½ tsp. salt	*Sift together.*
⅔ cup butter or margarine	*Cut into flour until particles are fine. Use pastry blender.*
1 egg, slightly beaten 1 tsp. vanilla	*Combine. Add to above, stir with wooden spoon until dough is moist enough to hold together.*
2 cups ground almonds ⅔ cup granulated sugar 1 tblsp. grated orange rind ½ cup orange juice 1 tblsp. lemon juice	*Combine and use as filling on rolled-out dough.*

SPECIAL INSTRUCTIONS: Roll out half of dough on 13 by 9-inch piece of waxed paper; roll to edges of paper. Invert into greased pan of same size and remove paper. Roll out remainder of dough on another 13 by 9-inch piece of waxed paper and set aside. Spread the almond filling over the dough in pan. Place remaining dough over filling; remove paper. Press lightly with spatula. Prick generously with fork. Bake.

Oven Temperature: 375 degrees Fahrenheit.

Baking Time: 25 to 30 minutes.

Frost immediately with Fancy Orange Icing (Page 304). Let stand for several hours and cut in bars or small squares.

Makes 21 large bars, or 42 squares.

CURRANT BARS

INGREDIENTS	METHOD
⅔ cup margarine	*Cream.*
1 cup brown sugar	*Add gradually and cream together well.*
1 egg 1 egg yolk	*Beat, blend in and mix well.*
2 cups all-purpose flour 1 tsp. powdered cinnamon 1 tsp. salt ½ tsp. baking soda	*Sift together. Add to the above and mix thoroughly.*
1½ cups dried currants ½ cup chopped nuts	*Soak currants, drain. Stir in with nuts.*
1 egg white 2 tblsps. sugar ¼ tsp. powdered cinnamon	*Before baking combine egg white, sugar and cinnamon. Beat slightly. See baking instructions below.*
Sliced nuts	*Sprinkle over cookies before baking.*

SPECIAL INSTRUCTIONS: Divide dough into 4 equal parts; shape each into a roll 12 inches long. Place 4 inches apart on greased cookie pans. Flatten to ½-inch thickness with floured fork. Brush with the mixture of egg white, sugar and cinnamon. Sprinkle with sliced nuts. Bake.

Oven Temperature: 400 degrees Fahrenheit.

Baking Time: 12 minutes.

Let cool; cut into 1-inch bars.

Makes 48 bars.

MAPLE BAR COOKIES

INGREDIENTS	METHOD
½ cup butter or shortening 1 cup brown sugar	*Cream well, adding sugar gradually.*
2 eggs ½ tsp. vanilla 1 tsp. maple flavoring	*Beat eggs, add to above, mix thoroughly.*
3 cups all-purpose flour ½ tsp. baking soda ¼ tsp. salt	*Sift together. Add slowly to egg mixture and blend until smooth.*

SPECIAL INSTRUCTIONS: Bake in lightly greased 8 by 12-inch pan.

Oven Temperature: 400 degrees Fahrenheit.

Baking Time: 8 to 10 minutes.

Let cool slightly. Cut into bars.

Makes 24 to 48 bars.

GOLDEN NUT BARS

INGREDIENTS	METHOD
1½ cups granulated sugar ¾ cup brown sugar 2 cups all-purpose flour ½ cup butter	*Mix with fork or pastry blender until all is fine crumbs.*
1 cup coarsely chopped nuts	*Sprinkle nuts in bottom of ungreased 13 by 9-inch pan, cover with 2 cups of above crumbs.*
1 egg ¾ tsp. salt ¾ tsp. grated nutmeg ¼ tsp. ground allspice 1 tsp. baking soda 1 cup sour milk or buttermilk	*Beat together until smooth. Stir into remaining crumbs.*

SPECIAL INSTRUCTIONS: Spread the egg mixture on top of crumbs in the pan. Bake.

Oven Temperature: 350 degrees Fahrenheit.

Baking Time: 45 minutes.

Let cool slightly, cut into 24 bars. The bottom layer should be firm but it will cut with sharp knife. Dust with confectioners' sugar.

Makes 24 bars.

HOLLYWOOD FRUIT BARS

INGREDIENTS	METHOD
¼ cup shortening	*Cream.*
½ cup fine granulated sugar	*Add gradually and mix well.*
1 egg	*Add and mix until fluffy.*
½ cup milk ⅓ cup molasses	*Mix milk and molasses together.*
2 cups all-purpose flour 1½ tsps. baking powder ¼ tsp. baking soda ¼ tsp. salt	*Sift together. Add ⅓ with the milk and molasses to the shortening mixture.*
½ cup chopped walnuts ½ cup seedless raisins, washed and drained ½ cup pitted dates, ground	*Add with remaining ⅔ of the flour mixture. Mix thoroughly.*

SPECIAL INSTRUCTIONS: Pour mixture into well greased and floured 10 by 15 by 1-inch cookie pan. Bake.

Oven Temperature: 325 degrees Fahrenheit.

Baking Time: 12 to 15 minutes.

Remove from oven and let cool. Cut in bars or squares and dip in granulated sugar.

Makes 35 bars or more squares.

INDIAN SQUARES

INGREDIENTS	METHOD
2 oz. (squares) un-sweetened chocolate ⅓ cup margarine	*Melt over boiling water in top of double boiler. Mix.*
2 eggs	*Beat well.*
1 cup granulated sugar	*Add to eggs gradually. Add chocolate and margarine. Blend well.*
¾ cup all-purpose flour ½ tsp. baking powder ½ tsp. salt	*Sift flour, baking powder and salt together. Add to chocolate mixture and mix thoroughly.*
1 tsp. vanilla ¾ cup chopped walnuts or pecans	*Add nuts with vanilla and blend together.*

SPECIAL INSTRUCTIONS: Bake in greased and floured 8 by 8-inch pan.

Oven Temperature: 350 degrees Fahrenheit.

Baking Time: 25 minutes or until done and slightly shrunken from sides of pan.

Remove from oven, let cool. Cover with Chocolate Frosting (Page 294). Cut into squares.

Makes 16 squares.

LAYER BARS

INGREDIENTS	METHOD
½ cup butter or margarine	*Melt and pour into a 9 by 13 by 2-inch pan.*
1 cup Graham Cracker crumbs	*Sprinkle a layer over the butter or margarine.*
3½ oz. (1 can) flaked coconut 6 oz. semi-sweet chocolate bits 6 oz. butterscotch bits 1 cup chopped nuts	*Combine and place on top of the crumbs.*
15 oz. (1 can) sweetened condensed milk	*Pour over and spread evenly.*

Oven Temperature: 350 degrees Fahrenheit.
Baking Time: 30 minutes.
While still warm cut into squares.
Makes 16 large bars.

*Indian
Squares*

MERINGUE BARS

INGREDIENTS	METHOD
2 egg whites ½ tsp. lemon juice	*Beat egg whites very stiff and dry. Beat in lemon juice or ¼ teaspoon cream of tartar.*
¼ cup fine, granulated sugar	*Add a spoonful at a time, beating until mixture holds its shape.*
½ tsp. vanilla	*Add and blend.*
¼ cup fine, granulated sugar	*Fold in gently and evenly.*
Pure food coloring	*See instructions below.*

SPECIAL INSTRUCTIONS: Color if desired with pure food coloring. Shape into bars with pastry bag and large plain tube, on a cookie pan covered with waxed paper. Bake.

Oven Temperature: 200 to 225 degrees Fahrenheit.

Baking Time: until meringues are very dry, 20 to 30 minutes; less if meringues are dry.

Remove from paper. If the meringues stick to the paper, wipe back of paper with a damp cloth. If baked in large pieces, break into smaller pieces and dust with confectioners' sugar.

Makes 10 or more bars.

NUT FINGERS

INGREDIENTS	METHOD
¾ cup shortening *	*Cream.*
½ cup fine, granulated sugar	*Add gradually, beat thoroughly.*
1 egg, well beaten 1 tsp. vanilla	*Add and blend.*
1 cup all-purpose flour ½ cup cornstarch ½ tsp. baking powder ½ tsp. salt	*Sift together.*
¼ cup finely ground nuts	*Add with sifted ingredients to shortening-sugar mixture. Stir well.*

SPECIAL INSTRUCTIONS: Use pastry bag and large tube. Form into finger lengths, about 1½ inches apart, on ungreased cookie pans. Bake.

Oven Temperature: 400 degrees Fahrenheit.

Baking Time: 10 to 12 minutes.

* Use half butter for flavor.

Makes 2 dozen or more strips.

NUT SQUARES

INGREDIENTS	METHOD
½ cup soft shortening 1 cup granulated sugar 1 egg 2 tsps. vanilla	*Beat shortening and sugar together until creamy. Add beaten egg and vanilla.*
1¾ cups all-purpose flour ½ tsp. baking soda ¾ tsp. salt	*Sift together, add to shortening mixture and blend until smooth.*
½ cup finely chopped nuts	*See instructions below.*

SPECIAL INSTRUCTIONS: Refrigerate dough for about 1 hour. Roll out ⅛ inch thick, cut into squares with a sharp knife and brush with milk. Use spatula and place about 1 inch apart on ungreased cookie sheet. Sprinkle each with some of the ½ cup finely chopped nuts. Bake.

Oven Temperature: 375 degrees Fahrenheit.

Baking Time: about 12 minutes or until golden brown.

Makes about 2 dozen squares.

RAISIN-NUT BARS

INGREDIENTS	METHOD
1 19-oz. package yellow-cake mix	*Pour half of cake mix into a bowl.*
¼ cup soft margarine ¼ cup brown sugar	*Cream margarine and sugar together.*
2 eggs, beaten ¼ cup water	*Combine with cake mix in bowl. Add water, beaten eggs and remaining cake mix.*
1 cup seedless raisins, washed and drained ¼ cup chopped pecans	*Blend thoroughly, stir in raisins and pecans evenly.*
1 egg white, beaten	*See* NOTE *below.*

SPECIAL INSTRUCTIONS: Turn dough into greased 13 by 9 by 2-inch pan. Bake.

Oven Temperature: 375 degrees Fahrenheit.

Baking Time: 30 minutes.

NOTE: Five minutes before removing from oven brush carefully with beaten egg white. Finish baking. Let cool. Cut into 2 by 1-inch bars.

Makes 18 large bars, or 24 squares.

SANDWICH BARS

INGREDIENTS	METHOD
⅓ cup evaporated milk 6 oz. (squares) bitter chocolate bits 3-oz. package cream cheese	*Combine milk and chocolate in top of double boiler and heat until chocolate melts, blend thoroughly. Do not boil. Remove from heat. Mix with cheese.*
¾ cup finely chopped nuts ½ tsp. vanilla	*Add and blend. Set this chocolate filling aside.*
½ cup margarine	*Cream.*
¾ cup granulated sugar	*Add gradually to margarine, cream well.*
2 egg yolks ¼ tsp. almond or orange extract	*Add to margarine mixture. Mix well.*
1½ cups all-purpose flour ½ tsp. baking powder ¼ tsp. salt	*Sift flour, baking powder and salt together and blend in thoroughly to the egg mixture.*
Pecan halves	*See instructions below.*

SPECIAL INSTRUCTIONS: Spread half of dough in a lightly greased 13 by 9 by 2-inch pan. Cover dough with the chocolate-cheese filling (which was set aside). Roll out remaining dough on floured surface to ⅛-inch thickness. Cut out with small cookie cutter. Place cut-out pieces on top of chocolate, spacing them evenly. Top each with a pecan half. Bake.

Oven Temperature: 375 degrees Fahrenheit.

Baking Time: 17 to 20 minutes.

Cut bars so pecan half is on each.

Makes 24 bars.

PECAN BUTTER FINGERS

INGREDIENTS	METHOD
½ cup butter 1 cup granulated sugar 2 eggs	*Cream butter and sugar together smoothly. Beat eggs into mixture.*
2 tblsps. light cream 1 tsp. almond extract	*Stir in and blend.*
2½ cups all-purpose flour ⅛ tsp. salt ¼ tsp. baking soda	*Sift together and add to butter-cream mixture. Mix until smooth.*
Finely chopped pecans	*See instructions below.*

SPECIAL INSTRUCTIONS: Cut dough into small pieces and roll by hand into finger-length rolls ½ inch wide. Dip each into finely chopped pecans. Place on lightly greased cookie pans. Bake.

Oven Temperature: 400 degrees Fahrenheit.

Baking Time: 8 minutes.

For PECAN STICKS make same dough but omit cream. Flavor with vanilla.

Makes about 4 dozen "fingers."

SPICE SQUARES

INGREDIENTS	METHOD
3 eggs 1 egg yolk	*Beat eggs and the extra yolk until thick and lemon colored.*
1½ cups brown sugar	*Add gradually, beat well.*
2¼ cups all-purpose flour ½ tsp. salt 1 tsp. baking powder ½ tsp. ground cloves 1 tsp. powdered cinnamon	*Sift together.*
1 cup diced mixed preserved fruits 1 cup coarsely chopped walnuts	*Combine with flour mixture.*
½ cup strong coffee or sherry	*Add alternately with flour mixture to egg-sugar mixture. Beat well.*

SPECIAL INSTRUCTIONS: Turn into greased 15½ by 10½ by 1-inch jelly roll pan, spread batter ½ inch thick. Bake.

Oven Temperature: 375 degrees Fahrenheit.

Baking Time: 25 minutes or until cake tester comes out clean. Let cool. Frost with Sugar Glaze (Page 301). Mark in 2 by 2½-inch bars before glaze dries. Cut when dry.

Makes 35 squares.

TUTTI-FRUTTI OBLONGS

INGREDIENTS	METHOD
2 cups brown sugar 1 cup butter	*Cream together.*
2 eggs	*Add and beat well.*
3½ cups all-purpose flour 1 tsp. baking soda	*Sift together. Add to above.*
1 tsp. vanilla ½ cup chopped nuts ½ cup diced, candied fruit	*Add to above and mix thoroughly into a medium stiff dough.*

SPECIAL INSTRUCTIONS: Press into 9-inch square pan lined with waxed paper or foil. Place in refrigerator for several hours. Cut in oblong slices. Bake.

Oven Temperature: 375 degrees Fahrenheit.

Baking Time: 20 to 25 minutes.

Makes 27 slices.

TASTY BROWN-SUGAR SQUARES

INGREDIENTS	METHOD
¼ cup butter	*Melt over low heat.* *Remove from heat.*
1 cup brown sugar	*Stir in and let cool.*
1 egg	*Beat and mix into butter* *and sugar.*
¾ cup all-purpose flour 1 tsp. baking powder ½ tsp. salt	*Sift together, stir in.*
½ tsp. vanilla ½ cup finely ground pecans	*Add and blend.*

SPECIAL INSTRUCTIONS: Spread in a well greased and floured square pan, 8 by 8 by 2 inches. Bake.

Oven Temperature: 350 degrees Fahrenheit.

Baking Time: about 25 minutes.

Cut into bars while still warm. Sift confectioners' sugar over them when cool.

Makes about 1½ dozen.

WALNUT SQUARES

INGREDIENTS	METHOD
¼ cup margarine 1 cup all-purpose flour ¼ tsp. salt	*Mix as when making streussel (coarse crumbs). Press into a 9 by 9 by 2-inch pan. Bake at 350 degrees Fahrenheit for 12 to 15 minutes.*
2 eggs ¾ cup granulated sugar	*While this crust bakes mix eggs with sugar.*
1 cup chopped walnuts ½ cup coconut flakes 1 tsp. almond extract ¼ tsp. salt 2 tblsps. all-purpose flour	*Add to egg mixture and blend well.*
2 tblsps. granulated sugar	*Sprinkle on top (see instructions).*

SPECIAL INSTRUCTIONS: Spread the nut-egg mixture over the partially baked bottom; sprinkle with granulated sugar and return to oven to finish baking.

Oven Temperature: 350 degrees Fahrenheit.

Baking Time: 15 minutes.

Cut into squares or bars.

Makes 18 or more squares.

TROPICAL BARS

BOTTOM DOUGH

INGREDIENTS	METHOD
½ cup margarine 1 cup granulated sugar 1 egg, beaten 1 tsp. vanilla ⅛ tsp. salt	*Mix together.*
1⅔ cups all-purpose flour	*Sift flour and mix into sugar-egg combination.*
Pineapple or raspberry jam	*See instructions below.*

SPECIAL INSTRUCTIONS: Spread this dough evenly in a 15 by 10 by 2-inch cookie pan. Brush the dough with a thin coating of pineapple or raspberry jam. Pierce with a fork in several places. Bake.

Oven Temperature: 375 degrees Fahrenheit.

Baking Time: 8 to 10 minutes.

FILLING

INGREDIENTS	METHOD
½ cup butter 1 cup brown sugar	*Cream together thoroughly.*
2 eggs	*Beat and mix well.*
1 cup all-purpose flour ½ tsp. baking powder ½ tsp. baking soda	*Sift together and add.*
½ cup quick cooking oatmeal ½ cup chopped coconut ¼ cup finely chopped pecans	*Blend in and mix thoroughly.*

SPECIAL INSTRUCTIONS: Cover the half-baked bottom of the Tropical Bars with this filling. Spread evenly and bake.
Oven Temperature: 400 degrees Fahrenheit.
Baking Time: about 12 minutes.
Let cool. Cut into bars.
Makes about 25 or more.

WALNUT BARS

INGREDIENTS	METHOD
⅓ cup butter or margarine ½ cup brown sugar	*Blend together and cream well.*
1⅓ cups all-purpose flour ½ tsp. baking powder	*Sift together and add. Mix with spoon or pastry blender until mixture resembles streussel (coarse crumbs).*
¼ cup finely ground walnuts	*Stir in, mix well.*

SPECIAL INSTRUCTIONS: Pat firmly into bottom of well greased 12 by 8 by 2-inch pan. Bake.

Oven Temperature: 350 degrees Fahrenheit.

Baking Time: 10 minutes ONLY.

WALNUT TOPPING	
2 eggs	*Beat until foamy.*
¼ cup light brown sugar ¾ cup dark corn syrup 3 tblsps. all-purpose flour ½ tsp. salt 1 tsp. vanilla	*Add sugar and syrup and mix well. Stir in flour, salt and vanilla.*
¾ cup finely chopped walnuts	*Sprinkle on top of above mixture (see instructions).*

SPECIAL INSTRUCTIONS: Pour over partially baked crust. Sprinkle with walnuts. Bake.

Oven Temperature: 350 degrees Fahrenheit.

Baking Time: 25 to 30 minutes.

Let cool in pan. Cut into bars.

Makes 32 bars.

3. BROWNIES

BASIC BROWNIES

INGREDIENTS	METHOD
1 cup sugar ¼ cup butter 1 egg	*Mix together until creamy.*
1 oz. (1 square) unsweetened chocolate ¾ tsp. vanilla	*Melt chocolate over hot water and add with vanilla to sugar mixture.*
½ cup all-purpose flour ½ cup chopped walnuts	*Immediately mix into the above, blend thoroughly.*

SPECIAL INSTRUCTIONS: Pour into waxed paper-lined 8- or 9-inch pan. (Grease the pan, line with waxed paper and grease the paper.) Bake.

Oven Temperature: 275 to 300 degrees Fahrenheit.

Baking Time: 30 minutes.

NOTE: After removing from oven, turn out on cake rack and peel paper off immediately to avoid its sticking. Cut in oblongs while still warm.

Makes 12 oblong brownies.

CHOCOLATE NUT BROWNIES

INGREDIENTS	METHOD
⅓ cup margarine 1 cup sugar 2 eggs	*Cream margarine, gradually mix in sugar and cream well. Add eggs, 1 at a time, beating after each.*
2 oz. (squares) unsweetened chocolate 2 tsp. vanilla ⅛ tsp. salt	*Melt chocolate over hot water, let cool, stir into egg mixture with vanilla and salt, mix thoroughly.*
⅔ cup all-purpose flour 1 cup chopped pecans	*Sift flour and add with ¾ cup pecans.*

SPECIAL INSTRUCTIONS: Spread evenly in greased and floured 9 by 9 by 2-inch pan. Sprinkle remaining ¼ cup pecans over top. If desired, all the pecans may be incorporated into the mixture, and after the brownies are baked and cooled the top may be frosted with Chocolate Icing (Page 292).

Oven Temperature: 350 degrees Fahrenheit.

Baking Time: 20 to 25 minutes.

Cut into bars or squares after icing has set.

Makes 16 large squares.

HAWAIIAN BROWNIES

INGREDIENTS	METHOD
½ cup butter or shortening 1 cup granulated sugar ¼ tsp. salt	*Cream together thoroughly.*
2 eggs	*Add, beat well.*
1 tsp. vanilla 2 oz. (squares) chocolate, melted 1 cup drained, canned crushed pineapple	*Add and mix together.*
1 cup all-purpose flour ½ tsp. baking powder ¼ tsp. baking soda ¼ cup chopped walnuts ¼ cup finely chopped or shredded coconut	*Sift flour with baking powder and soda, add with nuts and coconut to combined mixture. Mix thoroughly.*

SPECIAL INSTRUCTIONS: Bake in a buttered 9 by 9 by 2-inch pan.

Oven Temperature: 350 degrees Fahrenheit.

Baking Time: 35 minutes, approximately.

NOTE: Let cool in pan. Frost with Chocolate Icing (Page 292). After icing has set cut in squares.

Makes 25 large brownies.

SUGAR BROWNIES

INGREDIENTS	METHOD
2 eggs 1½ cups brown sugar ⅓ cup soft butter 1 tsp. vanilla	*Beat eggs until light,* *gradually add sugar, beat* *in soft butter and vanilla.*
1½ cups all-purpose flour 1 tsp. baking powder ¼ tsp. baking soda ½ tsp. salt 1 cup coarsely chopped nuts	*Sift flour, baking powder,* *soda and salt over nuts,* *mix well. Fold all into* *sugar mixture.*

SPECIAL INSTRUCTIONS: Bake in 12 by 8-inch shallow pan, greased and lined with greased waxed paper.

Oven Temperature: 375 degrees Fahrenheit.

Baking Time: 30 to 35 minutes.

Let cool on rack. Remove paper as soon as turned out of pan. Cut in squares or bars. Roll each in granulated or confectioners' sugar, if desired.

Makes 24 to 48 brownies.

Hawaiian Brownies

COUNTRY-HOUSE BROWNIES

INGREDIENTS	METHOD
⅓ cup soft butter 1 cup brown sugar 1 egg ¼ tsp. salt	*Cream butter with sugar, add egg and salt.*
¾ cup all-purpose flour 1 tsp. baking powder ¼ cup cocoa powder ½ tsp. vanilla	*Sift flour, baking powder and cocoa powder together. Add to the butter mixture with vanilla. Blend thoroughly.*
½ cup shredded or finely chopped coconut 6 oz. (squares) chocolate, grated or chopped ¼ cup nuts, sliced or chopped	*Add coconut and chocolate to the batter. Mix well.*

SPECIAL INSTRUCTIONS: Spread thinly in greased and floured 17 by 11-inch pan. Sprinkle batter with the nuts. Bake.

Oven Temperature: 350 degrees Fahrenheit.

Baking Time: 15 to 20 minutes.

NOTE: Cut in desired shapes after baking.

Makes about 40 pieces.

FRUIT CHOCOLATE BROWNIES

INGREDIENTS	METHOD
1 19-oz. package white-cake mix ½ cup (or slightly more) milk	*Empty cake mix into bowl, add milk and beat 1 minute.*
⅓ cup brown sugar 3 oz. (squares) unsweetened chocolate ½ cup pitted, finely chopped dates ¼ cup finely chopped candied cherries ½ cup chopped walnuts	*Add sugar gradually. Add melted chocolate, fruit and nuts. Mix well.*

SPECIAL INSTRUCTIONS: Spread in greased 9 by 9 by 2-inch pan lined with greased waxed paper. Bake.

Oven Temperature: 350 degrees Fahrenheit.

Baking Time: 30 to 35 minutes.

Turn baked brownies over on cake rack to cool. Peel off paper, turn right side up. Cut in squares or finger lengths. Roll in confectioners' sugar. Or frost with Chocolate Frosting before cutting (Page 294).

Makes about 25 squares.

SPEEDY BROWNIES

INGREDIENTS	METHOD
⅓ cup margarine 2 oz. (squares) un- sweetened chocolate 2 eggs	*Melt margarine and choco- late together over hot water. Remove from heat. Add eggs 1 at a time, beat well.*
1 cup granulated sugar 1 tblsp. corn syrup 1 tsp. vanilla	*Add and stir well.*
¾ cup all-purpose flour ½ tsp. baking powder ½ tsp. salt ⅔ cup chopped pecans	*Sift flour with baking powder and salt. Add to chocolate mixture with pecans, blend thoroughly.*

SPECIAL INSTRUCTIONS: Grease an 8 or 9-inch square pan, line with waxed paper and grease the paper. Pour batter in. Bake.

Oven Temperature: 350 degrees Fahrenheit.

Baking Time: 30 to 35 minutes.

Makes 16 or more brownies.

4. BUTTERSCOTCH, CARAMEL AND MAPLE COOKIES

BUTTERSCOTCH-CHIP COOKIES

INGREDIENTS	METHOD
⅔ cup margarine 1 cup brown sugar 1 egg 1 tsp. vanilla	*Cream margarine and sugar together, add egg and vanilla and blend.*
1½ cups all-purpose flour ½ tsp. baking soda ½ tsp. salt	*Sift together, blend into the above mixture.*
½ cup chopped nuts 6 oz. butterscotch pieces or chips	*Crush or break butterscotch fine. Add with nuts to dough.*

SPECIAL INSTRUCTIONS: Drop rounded teaspoons of dough about 2 inches apart on lightly greased cookie pans. Bake.

Oven Temperature: 375 degrees Fahrenheit.
Baking Time: 8 to 10 minutes or until delicately browned.
Let cool slightly before removing from pan.
Makes 24 or more drop cookies.

CARAMEL COOKIES

INGREDIENTS	METHOD
1 cup margarine ½ cup brown sugar 1 cup granulated sugar	*Cream margarine, adding sugars gradually until well blended.*
2 eggs 2 tsps. vanilla	*Beat eggs and add with vanilla.*
3¾ cups all-purpose flour 1 tsp. salt ½ tsp. baking soda	*Sift flour with salt and soda. Gradually add to the creamed mixture, mixing well.*

SPECIAL INSTRUCTIONS: Put dough through a cookie press and form rosettes on ungreased cookie pans. Dip a finger in cold water and make an indentation in the center of each cookie. Bake.

Oven Temperature: 400 degrees Fahrenheit.

Baking Time: 10 to 12 minutes.

When baked and cooled, fill the indentation with Caramel Icing (Page 306).

Makes about 70 to 80 cookies.

MAPLE-RUM-BUTTER COOKIES

INGREDIENTS	METHOD
1 cup butter or margarine ¾ cup sugar	*Cream butter or margarine and sugar together until light.*
3 egg yolks ½ tsp. vanilla ¼ tsp. almond extract 1½ tblsps. rum or rum flavoring	*Beat eggs, add flavorings and add to butter mixture.*
2½ cups all-purpose flour	*Sift flour, gradually add, and knead until smooth.*
3 to 4 tblsps. finely ground or powdered dried orange peel ¼ cup sugar	*See instructions below.*

SPECIAL INSTRUCTIONS: Shape in 2 long rolls about 2 inches in diameter, wrap in waxed paper and place in refrigerator overnight. To bake, cut in ¼ inch slices and roll each slice by hand to form a ball. Combine orange peel and ¼ cup sugar. Roll balls in this mixture. Place on cookie pans and flatten each ball with a tumbler dipped in the orange-sugar mixture.

Oven Temperature: 375 degrees Fahrenheit.

Baking Time: 10 to 12 minutes.

When baked decorate center of each cookie with a large, thick dot of Maple-Nut Icing (Page 299). Let cool. Store in an airtight container for a day or two to bring out the rum flavor.

Makes 40 or more cookies.

BUTTERSCOTCH COOKIES

INGREDIENTS	METHOD
2 cups brown sugar 1 cup butter 2 eggs	*Cream butter and sugar together well. Beat in eggs.*
3½ cups all-purpose flour 1 tsp. baking soda	*Sift flour and soda together and add to butter mixture.*
1 tsp. vanilla 1 cup finely chopped nuts or seedless raisins, washed and drained	*Add and mix until blended.*

SPECIAL INSTRUCTIONS: Form dough into 2 oblong bars. Wrap in waxed paper and place in refrigerator for several hours. To bake, slice very thin, place on greased and floured cookie sheets.

Oven Temperature: 400 degrees Fahrenheit.

Baking Time: 8 to 10 minutes.

Makes from 60 to 100 cookies.

5. CHOCOLATE COOKIES

CHINESE COOKIE BALLS

INGREDIENTS	METHOD
1 cup semi-sweet chocolate bits	*Melt over hot water. Remove from heat.*
3 tblsps. corn syrup 2 cups confectioners' sugar 1 cup finely chopped walnuts 2 tsps. instant coffee powder ½ cup hot milk 1¾ cups Graham Cracker crumbs 1 tsp. vanilla	*Add corn syrup and sugar and mix. Combine coffee powder and milk and stir in; add nuts, crumbs and flavoring. Mix well.*

SPECIAL INSTRUCTIONS: Shape into balls about the size of a walnut. Roll balls in confectioners' sugar. Chill.

NOTE: Fruit juice, brandy, rum or a liqueur may be used for half of the milk, but the cookies will then taste of the new ingredient and less of the mocha or coffee.

Makes 70 or more balls.

ASSORTED TEA COOKIES

INGREDIENTS	METHOD
¾ cup margarine ½ cup granulated sugar ½ tsp. salt	*Cream together well.*
1 egg	*Add and mix thoroughly.*
1 tsp. vanilla ½ tsp. almond extract	*Add and blend in.*
1¾ cups all-purpose flour 1 tsp. baking powder	*Sift flour and baking powder together, add to egg mixture and beat only until smooth.*
2 oz. (squares) un- sweetened chocolate 3 tblsps. confectioners' sugar	*Melt chocolate over hot water, add sugar and add this to ½ of the dough.*

SPECIAL INSTRUCTIONS: Divide dough in half and add the chocolate and confectioners' sugar to 1 half. Mix until blended. Press the other half of the dough through a cookie press onto ungreased cookie pan. Follow immediately with chocolate mix, squeezing it on top of the white cookies. Bake.

Oven Temperature: 375 degrees Fahrenheit.

Baking Time: 8 to 10 minutes.

Before baking, if desired, top each cookie with a glazed candied cherry, a small piece of candied pineapple, a blanched almond or pecan half, a few chocolate shots or a little grated coconut.

Makes 3 dozen or more.

BRAN-FLAKE CHIP MOUNTIES

INGREDIENTS	METHOD
¾ cup margarine	*Cream thoroughly.*
1 cup brown sugar	*Add gradually and cream together.*
2 eggs 1 tsp. vanilla	*Add 1 egg at a time; mix well after each.*
1¼ cups all-purpose flour 1 tsp. baking powder ¼ tsp. salt	*Stir in vanilla. Sift flour, baking powder and salt together and mix with the egg combination.*
¼ cup milk	*Add to egg combination alternately with flour.*
½ cup chopped pecans 3 cups bran flakes 7 oz. (squares) semi-sweet chocolate	*Cut chocolate in tiny pieces; stir in with flakes and nuts. Blend thoroughly.*

SPECIAL INSTRUCTIONS: Drop from teaspoon onto buttered cookie pan. Bake.

Oven Temperature: 375 degrees Fahrenheit.

Baking Time: 12 minutes or until done.

When cool, sift confectioners' sugar over lightly.

NOTE: Bittersweet chocolate may be used. Also semi-sweet chocolate bits may replace the chocolate squares.

Makes 50 to 60 mounties.

CHOCOLATE LOGS AND FANCIES

INGREDIENTS	METHOD
½ cup shortening ½ cup sugar	*Cream together until light.*
1 egg	*Beat in, mix well.*
1 oz. (square) un- sweetened chocolate 1 tblsp. cream 1 tsp. vanilla	*Melt chocolate over hot water, combine with cream and vanilla, add to egg mixture.*
¼ tsp. salt 2 cups all-purpose flour	*Sift together and blend into chocolate mixture.*

SPECIAL INSTRUCTIONS: Use cookie press or pastry bag and tube. Form cookies on ungreased cookie pans into 2-inch long bars, or 1½-inch rounds. Bake.

Oven Temperature: 400 degrees Fahrenheit.

Baking Time: 8 to 10 minutes.

Let cool. Put round cookies together in pairs with raspberry preserve and sprinkle with confectioners' sugar. Dip ends of bars in hot currant jelly, place on waxed paper and cover with finely chopped nuts or chocolate shots. Let cool.

Makes 2 to 3 dozen logs or small cookies.

CHOCOLATE DIPS

INGREDIENTS	METHOD
½ cup butter or margarine	*Cream well.*
¾ cup brown sugar	*Add gradually and cream together.*
¼ cup cream 2 tsps. instant coffee powder ¼ tsp. black walnut flavoring	*Combine and add to above and blend.*
2 cups all-purpose flour ½ tsp. baking powder ½ tsp. salt	*Sift together and add gradually to above, mix well.*

SPECIAL INSTRUCTIONS: Chill at least 1 hour. Shape with your fingers into sticks about 2 inches long and ½ inch in diameter. Place on ungreased cookie pan. Bake.

Oven Temperature: 375 degrees Fahrenheit.

Baking Time: 12 to 15 minutes.

Let cool. Dip 1 end of each stick into Chocolate Frosting (Page 294), then into ¼ cup nuts, finely chopped or ground. Let dry on waxed paper.

NOTE: If frosting becomes too stiff, reheat over hot water until usable.

Makes 3 to 4 dozen sticks.

CHOCOLATE-SOUR CREAM ROSETTES

INGREDIENTS	METHOD
1 cup shortening 1 cup sugar	*Cream together until smooth.*
1 egg ½ cup sour cream	*Beat egg, add with sour cream to sugar mixture. Beat until light and fluffy.*
¼ tsp. vanilla	*Stir in.*
3-3¼ cups all-purpose flour ½ tsp. salt ¼ tsp. baking powder ¼ tsp. baking soda 1 oz. (1 square) unsweetened chocolate	*Melt chocolate over hot water. Sift dry ingredients and add both to egg mixture. Blend.*

SPECIAL INSTRUCTIONS: Force through pastry bag with small star tube or use cookie press, onto ungreased cookie pans. Bake.

Oven Temperature: 375 degrees Fahrenheit.

Baking Time: 10 to 12 minutes.

Makes 3 to 4 dozen rosettes.

CHOCOLATE OBLONGS

INGREDIENTS	METHOD
¼ cup butter ¼ cup margarine	*Cream together.*
1 cup sugar	*Add gradually, beating well.*
1 egg 2 tblsps. milk 1 tsp. almond extract	*Add and mix together.*
2 oz. (squares) un- sweetened chocolate	*Melt chocolate over hot water. Let cool, add to egg mixture and mix thoroughly.*
2 cups all-purpose flour ½ tsp. salt	*Sift flour and salt together, add gradually, mix well.*

SPECIAL INSTRUCTIONS: Press through cookie press, or use pastry bag with large star tube, onto ungreased cookie pans, into 2-inch oblong shapes. Bake.

Oven Temperature: 350 degrees Fahrenheit.

Baking Time: 7 to 9 minutes.

Makes about 3 dozen oblongs.

CHOCOLATE BEAUTIES

INGREDIENTS	METHOD
½ cup shortening 1 cup brown sugar	*Cream together.*
1 egg	*Add and blend well.*
2 oz. (squares) un- sweetened chocolate	*Melt chocolate over hot water, let cool. Add to sugar mixture.*
1¾ cups all-purpose flour ½ tsp. baking soda ¼ tsp. salt	*Sift flour, baking soda and salt together.*
½ cup light cream	*Add alternately with sifted mixture to sugar mixture.*
1 tsp. vanilla 1 cup chopped pecans	*Add and blend well.*

SPECIAL INSTRUCTIONS: Drop from a teaspoon onto un-greased cookie pan. Bake.

Oven Temperature: 375 degrees Fahrenheit.

Baking Time: 8 to 10 minutes.

When cool, frost with Chocolate Frosting (Page 294).

Makes 60 or more cookies.

CHOCOLATE DOLITTLES

INGREDIENTS	METHOD
¼ cup butter ¾ cup brown sugar	*Cream together.*
1 egg 1 oz. (1 square) un- sweetened chocolate ¼ tsp. salt	*Melt chocolate over hot water and add with egg and salt to butter mixture. Mix thoroughly.*
¼ cup milk ½ tsp. vanilla	*Add to above alternately with flour.*
1 cup all-purpose flour 1 tsp. baking powder	*Sift with baking powder.*
¼ cup chopped walnuts	*Add and mix until all ingredients are blended.*

SPECIAL INSTRUCTIONS: Drop by teaspoon onto lightly greased cookie pans. Bake.

Oven Temperature: 350 degrees Fahrenheit.

Baking Time: 8 to 10 minutes.

Makes 2 dozen or more.

HAZEL'S CHOCOLATE CHIPS

INGREDIENTS	METHOD
½ cup shortening or butter ½ cup brown sugar ¼ cup granulated sugar	*Cream butter and both sugars until light.*
1 egg 1 tblsp. water ½ tsp. vanilla	*Beat egg, add with water and vanilla and blend.*
1¼ cups all-purpose flour ⅛ tsp. salt ½ tsp. baking soda	*Sift together and combine with egg-sugar mixture.*
1 6-oz. package chocolate chips	*Add to flour mixture.*

SPECIAL INSTRUCTIONS: Drop from teaspoon 2 inches apart on greased and lightly floured cookie pan. Bake.

Oven Temperature: 350 degrees Fahrenheit.

Baking Time: 10 minutes, approximately.

Makes 30 to 40 cookies.

CHOCOLATE BUTTER BALLS

INGREDIENTS	METHOD
1 cup butter 3 tblsps. confectioners' sugar	*Cream together.*
1 cup all-purpose flour 2 tsps. cocoa powder	*Sift together, add to above.* *Mix completely.*
½ cup chopped pecans 1 tsp. almond extract ½ tsp. milk, or more	*Add to cocoa mixture to* *make a medium stiff dough.*

SPECIAL INSTRUCTIONS: Place in refrigerator to chill. When chilled form into small balls, place on ungreased cookie pan. Bake.

Oven Temperature: 400 degrees Fahrenheit.

Baking Time: 8 to 10 minutes.

Makes 24 or more balls.

Hazel's Chocolate Chips

DELUXE CHOCOLATE-CHIP COOKIES

INGREDIENTS	METHOD
¾ cup brown sugar ½ cup butter	*Cream together.*
1 egg	*Beat egg, add and mix well.*
½ tsp. baking soda ½ tsp. salt 1 tsp. vanilla	*Blend in.*
1 cup all-purpose flour 1 6-oz. package chocolate chips ½ cup chopped pecans	*Sift flour. Add with chocolate chips and nuts and mix thoroughly.*

SPECIAL INSTRUCTIONS: Drop from teaspoon 2 inches apart on greased and lightly floured cookie pan. Bake.

Oven Temperature: 375 degrees Fahrenheit.

Baking Time: 10 to 12 minutes.

Makes about 32 cookies.

CHOCOLATE MOUNDS

INGREDIENTS	METHOD
½ cup butter 1 cup sugar	*Cream together until light and fluffy.*
3 eggs ½ tsp. vanilla	*Add and beat well.*
2 cups all-purpose flour 2 tsps. baking powder ½ tsp. baking soda 1 tsp. salt ½ cup cocoa powder	*Sift together.*
1 cup buttermilk or sour milk	*Add alternately with sifted ingredients to the butter-sugar mixture.*

SPECIAL INSTRUCTIONS: Drop by teaspoon onto ungreased cookie pans. Bake.

Oven Temperature: 350 degrees Fahrenheit.

Baking Time: 12 to 15 minutes.

Let cool. Cover top with Chocolate Icing (Page 292).

Makes 30 or more mounds.

CHOCOLATE STRASBURGERS

INGREDIENTS	METHOD
½ cup shortening	*Cream.*
½ cup sugar	*Add gradually, cream well.*
1 egg 1 tsp. vanilla	*Beat egg, add vanilla, and blend into sugar mixture.*
1½ cups all-purpose flour ¼ tsp. salt	*Sift together and blend in.*
2 oz. (squares) un- sweetened chocolate	*Melt chocolate over hot water. Mix in and blend thoroughly.*

SPECIAL INSTRUCTIONS: Press dough through cookie press. Use saw-toothed (spritz) plate, and make strips across ungreased cookie pan. Bake.

Oven Temperature: 400 degrees Fahrenheit.

Baking Time: 6 to 8 minutes.

While still warm cut into pieces about 2 inches wide and 2½ inches long, and remove from pan.

Makes about 2 dozen cookies.

CHOCOLATE LUMPS

INGREDIENTS	METHOD
1 cup milk	*Measure into saucepan.*
½ cup margarine	*Add and heat almost to boiling point. Remove from heat.*
1 cup all-purpose flour ¼ tsp. salt ¼ cup sugar	*Sift together, add all at once, stir constantly. Return to heat, cook until mixture leaves side of pan in smooth ball. Remove from heat.*
4 eggs	*Add 1 egg at a time. Beat well after each addition.*
1½ tsps. vanilla	*Blend in, mix well.*
3 oz. chocolate bits	*See instructions below.*

SPECIAL INSTRUCTIONS: Drop dough by half teaspoons 2 inches apart, onto ungreased cookie pans. Place 1 chocolate bit on each cookie. Then cover with teaspoon of dough. Bake.

Oven Temperature: 375 degrees Fahrenheit.

Baking Time: 15 to 20 minutes.

Let cool. Sprinkle with confectioners' sugar, if desired.

Makes 24 or more lumps.

CHOCOLATE THINS

INGREDIENTS	METHOD
2 oz. (squares) un-sweetened chocolate ¼ cup margarine	*Melt over hot water. Remove from heat. Add margarine and blend.*
1 cup light brown sugar 2 eggs, beaten ⅛ tsp. salt ½ cup all-purpose flour ½ cup coarsely chopped walnuts 1 tsp. vanilla	*Add sugar and beaten eggs to above. Sift flour and salt together and combine with egg mixture. Add nuts and vanilla.*

SPECIAL INSTRUCTIONS: Spread evenly in shallow square or oblong pan, which has been greased, lined with waxed paper, and the paper greased. Bake.

Oven Temperature: 300 degrees Fahrenheit.

Baking Time: 40 to 45 minutes.

Cut in squares.

Makes about 1½ dozen squares.

GRAHAM CHOCOLATE COOKIES

INGREDIENTS	METHOD
1¼ cups Graham Cracker crumbs (or 20 crushed Graham Crackers) ½ cup finely chopped pecans 1 tblsp. brown sugar 1 6-oz. package semi-sweet chocolate pieces 1⅓ cups (1 can) sweetened condensed milk	*Combine all ingredients.*

SPECIAL INSTRUCTIONS: Pour into a buttered 8-inch square pan. Bake.

Oven Temperature: 350 degrees Fahrenheit.

Baking Time: 35 to 40 minutes.

Let cool five minutes and cut into bars or squares.

Makes about 20 squares.

CHOCOLATE STICKS

INGREDIENTS	METHOD
½ cup butter ½ cup granulated sugar	*Cream together until light.*
1 egg 1 tsp. vanilla	*Beat egg, add with vanilla and mix well.*
1½ cups all-purpose flour	*Sift and combine with egg mixture until smooth.*

SPECIAL INSTRUCTIONS: Press through a pastry bag with flat decorating tube or use cookie press, into finger-long sticks on ungreased cookie pans. Bake.

Oven Temperature: 385 degrees Fahrenheit.

Baking Time: 8 minutes.

Place 2 cookies together using your favorite jam or jelly. Dip ends in Quick Bittersweet Chocolate Toppings, melted (see Page 293), then into chocolate shots, shredded coconut, finely chopped or ground nuts, such as pistachio nuts or imitation pistachio nuts (Page 310).

Makes about 2 dozen double sticks.

NO-BAKE RUM BALLS

INGREDIENTS	METHOD
2½ cups crushed vanilla wafers 1 cup finely chopped walnuts 1 cup confectioners' sugar 2 tblsps. sifted cocoa powder ⅜ tsp. salt	*Mix all together.*
⅓ cup rum 2 to 3 tblsps. dark corn syrup	*Add and mix evenly until thoroughly combined.*

SPECIAL INSTRUCTIONS: Dip your fingers in confectioners' sugar and form rum mixture into balls. Place on waxed paper and let set at least 4 to 5 hours to mellow. Roll balls in confectioners' sugar again and they are ready to serve.

NOTE: These balls may be rolled in Rum Icing (Page 300) in place of (final) confectioners' sugar.

Makes 4 or 5 dozen balls.

FANCY CHOCOLATE COOKIES

INGREDIENTS	METHOD
½ cup butter 1 cup fine granulated sugar	*Cream together until light.*
2 egg yolks 2 tblsps. milk 1 tsp. vanilla	*Beat egg yolks, add, and mix well. Add milk and vanilla.*
2 oz. (squares) un-sweetened chocolate	*Melt chocolate over hot water. Let cool and add.*
2 cups all-purpose flour ¼ tsp. salt	*Sift together, add to chocolate mixture and blend until smooth.*

SPECIAL INSTRUCTIONS: Force through a cookie press in fancy shapes onto ungreased cookie pans. Bake.

Oven Temperature: 350 degrees Fahrenheit.

Baking Time: 8 to 10 minutes.

When baked and cooled, dip end, top or sides of each cookie into melted Bittersweet Chocolate Frosting (Page 291). Place on waxed paper to dry. Or decorate the tops with fine lines or fancy designs. Use a small tube with melted bittersweet chocolate.

Makes 3½ to 4 dozen.

6. COCONUT COOKIES

COCONUT CUP CAKES, MACAROONS AND SLICES

INGREDIENTS	METHOD
2 cups shredded coconut ½ cup granulated sugar 2 egg whites (variable) 2 tblsps. all-purpose flour	*Mix all ingredients together in a double boiler until warm. Do not boil. Remove from heat and use as described here.*

SPECIAL INSTRUCTIONS: For Coconut Cup Cakes, spoon warm mixture into paper-lined miniature cup-cake tins and bake. For Coconut Macaroons, drop mixture from a spoon onto cookie pan greased and lined with greased waxed paper. Bake.

For Coconut Slices, pour mixture into 8-inch square pan containing a thin layer of Sugar Cookie Dough (Page 308), which has been spread with raspberry jam. Bake.

Oven Temperature: 350 degrees Fahrenheit.

Baking Time: Until top is golden brown.

NOTE: Sugar Cookie Dough is listed under Plain Cookie Dough for Cookie Bottoms (Page 308).

Makes 16 miniature cup cakes, or 16 to 20 macaroons or 32 slices.

COCONUT-CHOCOLATE DROP COOKIES I

INGREDIENTS	METHOD
½ cup shortening	*Cream.*
1 cup brown sugar	*Add, continue creaming until light.*
1 egg	*Add and beat well.*
3 oz. (3 squares) unsweetened chocolate ¼ cup hot coffee	*Melt chocolate in hot coffee and let cool slightly. Add to egg-sugar mixture.*
2 cups all-purpose flour ½ tsp. salt ½ tsp. baking soda ⅔ cup thick sour cream (commercial)	*Sift flour, salt and soda together, then add alternately with the sour cream to the chocolate mixture.*
⅓ cup finely cut or shredded coconut	*Stir into the flour mixture.*

SPECIAL INSTRUCTIONS: Drop from a teaspoon onto a lightly greased cookie pan. Bake.

Oven Temperature: 375 degrees Fahrenheit.

Baking Time: 12 to 15 minutes.

Let cool, then store in a tightly covered container.

Makes 32 or more cookies.

COCONUT-CHOCOLATE DROP COOKIES II

INGREDIENTS	METHOD
2 oz. (squares) un-sweetened chocolate	*Melt over hot water.*
½ cup shortening 6 tblsps. brown sugar 6 tblsps. granulated sugar ½ tsp. vanilla 1 egg	*Add shortening and sugars to chocolate and cream together about 5 minutes. Add vanilla and beat egg in smoothly.*
1½ cups all-purpose flour ½ tsp. baking soda ½ tsp. salt	*Sift flour, soda and salt together, blend with above mixture for about 6 minutes.*
1 cup chopped or shredded coconut	*Add and mix in well.*

SPECIAL INSTRUCTIONS: Drop ½ teaspoons of the mixture on well-greased and floured cookie pans. Bake.

Oven Temperature: 350 degrees Fahrenheit.

Baking Time: about 9 minutes.

Let cool for 3 minutes and remove with spatula from cookie pan.

Makes about 40 cookies.

COCONUT BARETTES

INGREDIENTS	METHOD
½ cup granulated sugar ⅓ cup shortening	*Blend and then cream together 5 minutes.*
1 cup all-purpose flour	*Sift and add to above, mix lightly.*

SPECIAL INSTRUCTIONS: Press mixture into a 9 by 12-inch pan. Bake.
Oven Temperature: 350 degrees Fahrenheit.
Baking Time: 12 minutes.
Then cover with following Walnut Mixture.

WALNUT MIXTURE

2 eggs 1 cup granulated sugar	*Beat together until light.*
2 tblsps. all-purpose flour 1 tsp. baking powder	*Sift together and add to egg mixture.*
½ tsp. almond extract ½ tsp. vanilla ½ tsp. salt	*Add to egg-sugar-flour mixture.*
1 cup finely shredded coconut ¾ cup Rice Krispies 1½ cups chopped walnuts	*Combine and add to flour-egg mixture.*

SPECIAL INSTRUCTIONS: Spread walnut mixture over top of partially baked sugar-shortening-and-flour dough. Return to oven and continue baking.

Oven Temperature: 350 degrees Fahrenheit.

Baking Time: 20 to 25 minutes.

Let cool and cut as desired into strips or squares.

Makes 24 to 48 pieces.

COCONUT CRISPIES

INGREDIENTS	METHOD
¼ cup butter or margarine ½ cup brown sugar ¼ cup granulated sugar 1 egg ¼ tsp. vanilla	*Cream butter or margarine, add sugars and cream together about 3 minutes. Beat egg and add with vanilla.*
1 cup all-purpose flour ½ tsp. baking soda ¼ tsp. salt	*Sift flour, soda and salt together and add gradually to egg-sugar mixture.*
1 cup finely cut or shredded coconut 1 cup Wheaties (cereal)	*Mix in well with dry ingredients above.*

SPECIAL INSTRUCTIONS: Drop dough from teaspoon into little mounds on ungreased cookie pans. Bake.

Oven Temperature: 375 degrees Fahrenheit.

Baking Time: 8 to 10 minutes.

Makes about 40 cookies.

COCONUT DROPS

INGREDIENTS	METHOD
1¼ cups granulated sugar ⅔ cup butter (room temperature)	*Cream together well.*
2 eggs 1 tsp. rum or rum flavoring 1 tsp. vanilla	*Beat eggs, add with flavorings and cream well.*
⅔ cup drained, canned crushed pineapple ⅓ cup drained maraschino cherries	*Chop cherries fine and add with pineapple to the egg-sugar mixture.*
3 cups all-purpose flour 1 tsp. baking powder 1 tsp. baking soda 1 tsp. salt	*Sift flour, baking powder, soda and salt together and add to above.*
1 cup finely chopped nuts	*Add nuts to flour mixture and blend completely.*
1½ cups chopped or shredded coconut	*See instructions below.*

SPECIAL INSTRUCTIONS: Drop by rounded teaspoon onto greased cookie pans. Bake.

Oven Temperature: 375 degrees Fahrenheit.

Baking Time: 15 minutes, approximately.

Let cookies cool and then dip each in Pineapple Icing (Page 303). Then dip into chopped or shredded coconut. Let dry.

Makes about 80, or more, cookies.

COCONUT SUGAR GEMS

INGREDIENTS	METHOD
1 cup butter	*Cream.*
2 cups granulated sugar	*Add sugar gradually to butter and cream together.*
2 whole eggs (or 4 yolks) 1 tsp. vanilla	*Mix in.*
¾ tsp. salt 2 tsps. baking powder 3¼ cups all-purpose flour	*Sift together.*
2 tblsps. cream or milk	*Add alternately with flour mixture to egg-sugar mixture.*
Sugar Shredded or chopped coconut	*Sprinkle on top (see instructions).*

SPECIAL INSTRUCTIONS: Roll to about ⅛ inch thickness on lightly floured surface. Cut with medium sized cookie cutter. Place on cookie pans, brush lightly with water and sprinkle with a mixture of sugar and coconut. Bake.

Oven Temperature: 375 degrees Fahrenheit.

Baking Time: 10 to 12 minutes.

NOTE: Equal amounts of sugar and finely chopped nuts make a good combination to sprinkle on top of the cookies in place of the sugar and coconut mixture.

Makes about 3 dozen cookies.

7. CONES, CORNUCOPIAS, CRESCENTS—"HORNS"

ALMOND CRESCENTS OR HORNS

INGREDIENTS	METHOD
1 cup granulated sugar 1 cup butter	*Cream together well.*
1 egg 1 tsp. almond extract	*Add and mix.*
2¼ cups cake flour	*Sift.*
2 cups ground almonds	*Mix with sifted flour, add to egg mixture and make a fairly stiff dough.*

SPECIAL INSTRUCTIONS: Spoon out small pieces, and roll each with fingers into crescent shape (called a horn by European pastry makers). Bake on ungreased cookie pans.

Oven Temperature: 375 degrees Fahrenheit.

Baking Time: 10 minutes or until a light brown color.

When cool, dust crescents with confectioners' sugar.

Makes 4 dozen or more.

CORNUCOPIAS

INGREDIENTS	METHOD
1 egg	*Beat slightly in small deep bowl.*
⅓ cup confectioners' sugar	*Add and continue beating until very thick.*
2 tblsps. water	*Add gradually, beat until thick and light.*
½ cup cake flour	*Measure sifted flour and sift again. Add all at once and fold in with spoon until just blended.*

SPECIAL INSTRUCTIONS: Grease cookie pan and dust with flour. Turn pan upside down and tap pan to remove any excess flour. Drop cookie dough from tablespoon into pan, spreading each cookie with a spoon into a very thin 5-inch circle. (It is best to bake only 3 cookies at a time so they may be rolled while still warm over a large wooden spoon handle.)

Oven Temperature: 350 degrees Fahrenheit.

Baking Time: 10 minutes or until golden brown.

Remove each cookie from pan with spatula and roll at once into a cone. If necessary, place cookie pan over low heat or return to oven for 1 or 2 minutes in order to remove cookies easily. When cornucopias are cold, fill with Strawberry Whipped Cream (Page 307). Serve at once.

Makes about 30 cornucopias.

FRESH STRAWBERRY CORNETS

INGREDIENTS	METHOD
¼ cup butter ¼ cup granulated sugar	*Cream together.*
⅓ cup all-purpose flour ¼ tsp. salt	*Sift together, add to above.*
1 egg	*Beat well, add to above.* *Mix until smooth.*

Fresh sliced, sugared
    Strawberry Whip fill-
    ing (page 307)
Whipped cream or light
    Butter Cream Icing
    (page 289)
Nuts, finely chopped
	See instructions below.

SPECIAL INSTRUCTIONS: Drop batter from teaspoon onto well greased cookie pan. Spread into rounds 3 to 4 inches in diameter. Bake.

Oven Temperature: 400 degrees Fahrenheit.

Baking Time: 7 to 10 minutes, or until brown around the edges. Remove from pan with spatula and while still warm shape each into a cylinder around the handle of a large wooden spoon. Remove and let cool. To serve, fill with Strawberry Whip filling (Page 307). Decorate ends with a dab of whipped cream or Butter-Cream Icing (Page 289). Dip in finely chopped nuts.

Makes about 40 cornets.

CRISPY THIN HOLLOWS

INGREDIENTS	METHOD
1⅔ cups granulated sugar ½ tsp. vanilla 5 egg whites ⅛ tsp. salt	*Beat together until egg whites are frothy and thick.*
¾ cup melted margarine	*Add and mix well.*
1 cup all-purpose flour ⅔ cup finely ground almonds	*Blend in and mix until well incorporated.*

SPECIAL INSTRUCTIONS: Drop by teaspoon into heavily greased cookie shaped forms,* 5 to 6 inches apart. Spread the dough to fit the form. Bake.

Oven Temperature: 350 degrees Fahrenheit.

Baking Time: about 8 minutes.

Immediately and gently remove the "hollows" (as the thin pastry form is called) 1 at a time, so each can be molded immediately over a thin rolling pin or large wooden spoon handle before it cools. Bake only a few at a time. If they become too cool to mold, return to oven for 1 or 2 minutes. When cool fill with your favorite butter cream or lightly sweetened whipped cream.

* These leaf, tree, heart, etc., shaped forms, or stencils (as they are called by pastry chefs), are made of tin or cardboard and after the mixture has been spread in them, they are lifted up and used for the next "hollow."

Makes 50 or more hollows.

VIENNESE CRESCENTS OR HORNS

INGREDIENTS	METHOD
1 cup butter	*Cream.*
½ cup granulated sugar 2 cups all-purpose flour 1 cup ground almonds 1 tsp. vanilla	*Add sugar and mix thoroughly; add flour, almonds and flavoring. Mix together thoroughly.*
Confectioners' sugar	*See instructions below.*

SPECIAL INSTRUCTIONS: Spoon out small pieces of dough, shape with fingers into small horns or crescents about 3 inches long and 1 inch thick. Arrange on buttered cookie pans. Bake.

Oven Temperature: 325 degrees Fahrenheit.

Baking Time: 30 minutes.

While still warm roll each in confectioners' sugar. Let cool. Roll again in confectioners' sugar.

Makes 60 or more.

**Sugar Crescents
or Horns**

SUGAR CRESCENTS OR HORNS

INGREDIENTS	METHOD
½ cup butter 1 cup granulated sugar	*Cream together.*
2 egg yolks ½ tsp. lemon extract	*Add and beat until smooth.*
2 tblsps. sour milk or sweet milk 1¾ cups all-purpose flour 1 tsp. baking powder ⅛ tsp. baking soda ⅛ tsp. salt	*Sift flour, baking powder, soda and salt together. Add with milk to the egg mixture.*
Chopped nuts Granulated sugar Candied cherry pieces	*See instructions below.*

SPECIAL INSTRUCTIONS: Chill dough in refrigerator. Spoon out small amounts, roll in fingers and shape into crescents. Brush with milk, and roll each into mixture of chopped nuts and granulated sugar. Set a cherry piece in the center of each and bake.

Oven Temperature: 350 to 375 degrees Fahrenheit.

Baking Time: 15 minutes.

NOTE: Streussel can be substituted for chopped nuts and sugar mixture, if desired (Page 309).

Makes 70 or more crescents.

CRISP COOKIE ROLLS

INGREDIENTS	METHOD
⅓ cup molasses	*Heat almost to boiling point in saucepan, remove from heat.*
½ cup shortening	*Mix in until melted.*
1 cup all-purpose flour 3 tblsps. powdered milk ⅔ cup granulated sugar 1 tsp. ground ginger	*Sift together and add slowly. Blend.*

SPECIAL INSTRUCTIONS: Drop by half teaspoon, 4 inches apart, on well greased cookie pans. Bake.

Oven Temperature: 325 degrees Fahrenheit.

Baking Time: 10 to 14 minutes or until done.

Remove from oven; let stand 1 minute; then quickly loosen all cookies with sharp, broad knife or spatula. While cookies are still warm and pliable, roll, 1 at a time, around handle of wooden spoon. Slip off spoon and let cool on rack. Store in tightly covered container. Serve plain or filled with whipped cream.

NOTE: If cookies cool too much for rolling, return to oven for 1 or 2 minutes to soften.

Makes 60 or more.

CRISPY CONES

INGREDIENTS	METHOD
½ cup granulated sugar ½ cup butter or shortening	*Cream together until light.*
1 cup all-purpose flour	*Sift and add, mix smooth.*
4 egg whites 1 tsp. vanilla	*Beat until stiff, add vanilla and fold gently into mixture until well incorporated.*

SPECIAL INSTRUCTIONS: Have well greased or buttered pans ready. Drop 1 teaspoon of batter onto each one. Batter spreads to 4- or 5-inch circle. Make 3 on each pan. Bake 1 pan at a time.

Oven Temperature: 400 to 425 degrees Fahrenheit.

Baking Time: 10 to 12 minutes until golden brown.

Lift up each cookie with a spatula and quickly roll into a cone over the end of a thick wooden spoon handle or a cone-shaped wooden pastry form. Remove cone from handle after it holds its shape; this is about 1 to 2 minutes. Let cool. Fill cones with whipped cream just before serving.

Makes 90 or more cones.

LITTLE SUGAR-AND-NUT CRESCENTS

INGREDIENTS	METHOD
1 compressed yeast cake ¼ cup warm water	*Break up in water and soften.*
¾ cup margarine 2 egg yolks ¼ cup light cream ½ tsp. vanilla ½ tsp. almond extract	*Combine margarine, egg yolks, cream and flavorings.*
2½ cups all-purpose flour ¼ cup granulated sugar 1½ tsps. salt ½ cup chopped nuts	*Sift flour and sugar together. Blend into creamed mixture with softened yeast. Let stand at room temperature about 2 hours in bowl covered with towel.*
2 egg whites, slightly beaten 1 tblsp. water ¾ cup granulated sugar ¾ cup finely chopped pecans 2 tsps. instant coffee powder	*Combine egg whites and water. In a second bowl mix sugar, pecans and coffee powder.*

SPECIAL INSTRUCTIONS: Break off small pieces of dough and shape by hand into crescents. Dip crescents into the egg-white mixture. Then roll them in the sugar-coffee powder mixture. Place crescents on foil lined cookie pans. Bake.

Oven Temperature: 385 degrees Fahrenheit.

Baking Time: about 12 minutes.

Dust with sifted confectioners' sugar.

Makes about 40 crescents.

ALMOND WAFERS OR HOLLOWS

INGREDIENTS	METHOD
½ cup granulated sugar ½ cup butter	*Cream together until smooth. Heat, stirring in saucepan until butter melts.*
¾ cup finely ground almonds 1 tblsp. all-purpose flour 2 tblsps. light cream	*Add almonds and mix until smooth. Sift flour and add alternately with cream. Beat until well blended.*

SPECIAL INSTRUCTIONS: Drop by teaspoon onto well greased cookie pan, spreading thin, and at least 4 inches apart. Bake.

Oven Temperature: 250 degrees Fahrenheit.

Baking Time: until the edges are slightly brown.

Remove from oven and, while the wafers are still warm, as quickly as you can, form each around a stick or large wooden-spoon handle and press the edges together. Slip roll off onto a sheet of waxed paper. Let cool. Fill them with whipped cream.

Makes 4 to 5 dozen wafers.

8. FRUIT-FILLED COOKIES

BOSTON TEA CAKES

INGREDIENTS	METHOD
½ cup butter ¾ cup granulated sugar	*Mix together and cream well.*
1 egg	*Add and beat until fluffy.*
3 tblsps. milk ½ cup mixed chopped candied fruit ½ cup white raisins or currants	*Add and mix lightly.*
1¾ cups all-purpose flour 1½ tsps. baking powder 1 tsp. salt	*Sift together, add and mix until thoroughly blended.*

SPECIAL INSTRUCTIONS: With your fingers roll teaspoons of dough into 1-inch balls. Place on lightly greased cookie pans. Press lightly with spatula. Bake.

Oven Temperature: 375 degrees Fahrenheit.

Baking Time: about 15 minutes or until golden brown.

Makes 40 to 50 cookies.

CANDIED-FRUIT COOKIES

INGREDIENTS	METHOD
½ cup brown sugar ¼ cup butter	*Cream together until light.*
2 eggs	*Add and beat well.*
2 scant tsps. baking soda 2 tblsps. milk	*Combine, add and mix well.*
¼ cup rum or brandy	*Add and stir into mixture.*
1¼ cups all-purpose flour ½ tsp. powdered cinnamon ½ tsp. grated nutmeg ½ tsp. ground cloves ¼ tsp. salt	*Sift together, add to above, mix until smooth.*
¼ cup all-purpose flour 1 cup pecan halves ½ cup broken pecans 2 cups candied whole cherries 1 cup seedless raisins ½ cup chopped candied pineapple	*Dust fruits and nuts with flour, add to brandy dough and mix until well distributed.*

SPECIAL INSTRUCTIONS: Drop from teaspoon onto greased and floured cookie pans. Bake.

Oven Temperature: 300 degrees Fahrenheit.

Baking Time: 20 to 25 minutes, or until done.

Let cool. Ice with Chocolate Icing (Page 292), if desired.

Makes 90 or more cookies.

ASSORTED FILLED COOKIES

INGREDIENTS	METHOD
¾ cup butter 1 cup granulated sugar	*Cream together.*
2 eggs	*Add and mix until smooth.*
3½ cups all-purpose flour 2½ tsps. baking powder ½ tsp. salt	*Sift together, add alternating with milk and flavoring.*
⅓ cup milk ½ tsp. almond extract	*Combine and add with flour, above.*

SPECIAL INSTRUCTIONS: Roll out dough ⅛ inch thick on a floured pastry cloth. Cut with 2 to 3-inch round cookie cutter. Place cookies on greased cookie pans. Add 1 teaspoon prepared filling such as apricot, date, fig, prune or raisin. Cover each with another ⅛-inch-thick cookie. Press edges together with tines of fork. Brush each with milk, or a mixture of 1 egg, pinch of salt and 2 tablespoons milk. Bake.

Oven Temperature: 400 degrees Fahrenheit.

Baking Time: 12 to 15 minutes.

NOTE: Prepared fillings available in food stores can be used for these cookies. Also see filling recipes (Pages 287-88).

Makes about 1½ dozen filled cookies.

EASY-TO-MAKE COOKIES

INGREDIENTS	METHOD
½ cup butter ¼ cup granulated sugar ¼ tsp. salt 1 egg ½ tsp. almond extract	*Cream together in mixer for 2 minutes.*
1 cup all-purpose flour	*Sift and stir into above making a smooth dough.*
1 egg white 1 tblsp. water 1 cup chopped walnuts	*See instructions below.*
Raspberry jam	

SPECIAL INSTRUCTIONS: Roll rounded teaspoons of dough into balls. Dip each ball into egg white mixed with water and immediately roll in nuts. Place cookie balls 2 inches apart on lightly greased cookie pans. Press thumb in center of each cookie. Use raspberry jam to fill the thumb depression. Bake.

Oven Temperature: 375 degrees Fahrenheit.

Baking Time: about 10 minutes.

Makes 32 or more cookies.

DATE WHEELS

INGREDIENTS	METHOD
¾ cup pitted dates, finely cut	*Cover dates with boiling water, let stand 5 minutes. Drain. Cut fine with scissors.*
1 tblsp. all-purpose flour	*Coat dates with this flour.*
⅔ cup all-purpose flour ½ tsp. baking powder ½ tsp. salt	*Sift these dry ingredients together.*
3 eggs	*Beat until foamy.*
¾ cup granulated sugar	*Gradually add sugar to eggs, beat until thick and fluffy.*
½ tsp. vanilla	*Blend in. Fold in sifted dry ingredients carefully.*
½ cup finely chopped pecans	*Fold in with cut-up floured dates.*
20 maraschino cherries 1 tblsp. confectioners' sugar 1 cup finely chopped pecans	*See instructions below.*

SPECIAL INSTRUCTIONS: Grease a 15 by 11-inch jelly roll pan, line it with waxed paper, grease the paper generously and flour it lightly. Spread dough in pan. Drain cherries, arrange 10 cherries across each end of dough about ½ inch from edge of dough. Bake.

Oven Temperature: 325 degrees Fahrenheit.

Baking Time: 30 to 35 minutes, or less. Test for doneness.

Turn hot cake out onto waxed paper which has been sprinkled with 1 tablespoon confectioners' sugar. Remove the hot paper baked onto the bottom of the cake. Cut cake crosswise into 2 11 by 7½-inch rectangles. Roll up each rectangle tightly, beginning with the cherry end. Wrap in waxed paper and chill. Spread chilled rolls thinly with Butter-Cream Icing (Page 289), and roll in the chopped pecans. Chill again. To serve, cut in ¼ to ½-inch slices.

Makes about 20 to 40 cookies.

DATE DELIGHTS

INGREDIENTS	METHOD
¾ cup pitted dates, chopped ¼ cup granulated sugar ¼ cup water	*Combine in saucepan, cook until thickened, stirring constantly. Remove from heat.*
2 tsps. lemon juice ½ tsp. grated lemon rind ¼ cup finely chopped nuts	*Blend into date mixture.*
⅔ cup shortening 1¼ cups brown sugar 1½ tsps. grated orange rind	*Cream together until light.*
1 egg 1 tblsp. vinegar	*Beat into shortening mixture.*
2 cups all-purpose flour ¼ tsp. baking soda ¼ tsp. salt	*Sift together. Beat with shortening and egg mixture.*

SPECIAL INSTRUCTIONS: Chill dough several hours or overnight. Roll dough into 15 by 10-inch rectangle. Spread with date mixture. Starting from a long side, roll as for jelly roll. Make roll tight. Chill 1 hour. Slice into ¼-inch slices. Place on cookie pans and bake.

Oven Temperature: 375 degrees Fahrenheit.

Baking Time: 12 to 15 minutes or until lightly browned.

NOTE: Bought date fillings can be used.

Makes about 60 cookies.

DATE WINDWHEELS

INGREDIENTS	METHOD
½ cup shortening, part butter or margarine 1 cup brown sugar 1 egg ½ tsp. vanilla	*Cream butter and sugar together thoroughly. Beat in egg and vanilla.*
1¾ cups all-purpose flour ½ tsp. baking soda ¼ tsp. salt	*Sift together. Stir into egg mixture and mix thoroughly.*
½ cup Date-Nut Filling (See Page 310)	*See instructions below.*

SPECIAL INSTRUCTIONS: Divide dough in half. Roll each piece of dough on waxed paper into a rectangle about 11 by 7 inches. Spread each rectangle with ½ cup cooled Date-Nut Filling (Page 310). Roll up tightly, beginning at wide side. Pinch edges together to seal. Wrap each roll in waxed paper and chill several hours. Cut in ¼-inch slices. Place on lightly greased cookie pans. Bake.

Oven Temperature: 400 degrees Fahrenheit.

Baking Time: 10 minutes or until slightly brown.

For FIG WHEELS, substitute Fig Filling (Page 288) for the Date-Nut Filling.

Makes 60 to 70 or more cookies.

DATE MOUNDS, BARS AND CUP CAKES

INGREDIENTS	METHOD
1 cup sweetened condensed milk ⅓ cup (3 or 4) egg whites, beaten 4 cups finely shredded coconut 1 cup finely chopped nuts 1 cup chopped pitted dates 1 tsp. vanilla 1 tsp. almond extract	*Beat egg whites slightly. Combine smoothly with coconut, milk and remaining ingredients.*

SPECIAL INSTRUCTIONS: Drop by teaspoon onto well greased and floured cookie pans. Bake.

Oven Temperature: 350 degrees Fahrenheit.

Baking Time: 12 minutes, or until golden brown.

For Bars, spread dough in square or oblong pans. Bake. When cool, cut in bars. Bars can also be put together when cold with Rich Butter-Cream Frosting (Page 296). For Cup Cakes, spoon mixture into cup cake pans lined with pleated paper cups.

Makes about 48 bars (24 filled bars). Or makes 10 or more dozen small drop cookies. Or makes 21 to 28 cup cakes.

HAWAIIAN COOKIES

INGREDIENTS	METHOD
2¼ cups all-purpose flour 1 cup sugar ½ tsp. baking powder	*Sift together in a bowl.*
¾ cup butter	*Cut in until all is coarse crumbs.*
1 egg	*Beat slightly, add to crumbs and mix. Knead dough to mix well.*
Pineapple Filling	*See instructions below.*

SPECIAL INSTRUCTIONS: Divide dough into 30 even-sized pieces. Shape each piece into a ball, then flatten to ½ inch thickness. Place on cookie pan, dip a finger into cold water and make a small depression about the size of an almond in center of each cookie. Fill this with pineapple preserves, or any preferred fruit jam. Bake.

Oven Temperature: 325 degrees Fahrenheit.

Baking Time: 25 to 30 minutes.

NOTE: Add ¼ teaspoon almond extract or 1 teaspoon vanilla with the egg to the cookie dough, if desired.

Makes 30 cookies.

FRUIT-FILLED COOKIES

INGREDIENTS	METHOD
½ cup butter ½ cup margarine	*Cream.*
1¼ cups brown sugar	*Add to butter and margarine and cream until smooth.*
¼ cup dark corn syrup	*Blend in. Mix well.*
1 egg 1 tblsp. light cream	*Beat egg, combine with cream and add to sugar mixture.*
3 cups all-purpose flour 1 tsp. ground ginger ½ tsp. baking soda ½ tsp. instant coffee powder	*Sift together. Add to creamed mixture. Mix thoroughly.*
Apricot Filling	*See instructions below.*

SPECIAL INSTRUCTIONS: Roll out ⅓ of dough at a time on a floured board or pastry cloth to ⅛-inch thickness. Use 2½-inch cookie cutter and cut pastry into rounds. Place on ungreased cookie pans. Add ½ teaspoon of apricot or other fruit filling such as prune, raspberry, etc., to the center of each round. Fold dough over, press edges together making half-moon cookies. Bake.

Oven Temperature: 350 degrees Fahrenheit.

Baking Time: 12 to 15 minutes.

Makes about 60 to 70 cookies.

JAM-FILLED CINNAMON BUTTER COOKIES

INGREDIENTS	METHOD
1 cup butter	*Cream.*
1 cup brown sugar	*Gradually cream into butter.*
2 eggs, well beaten 1 tblsp. grated lemon rind 2 tblsps. lemon juice 1 tsp. powdered cinnamon ¼ tsp. ground cloves 2 cups all-purpose flour	*Add and mix. More flour may be needed to make a medium stiff dough. Blend well.*

SPECIAL INSTRUCTIONS: Chill dough. Roll thin, cut out with round cookie cutter and add a little jam to the center of each. Bake.

Oven Temperature: 350 degrees Fahrenheit.

Baking Time: about 10 minutes.

Makes 30 or more thin cookies.

Fruit-Filled Cookies

FRUIT-CAKE COOKIES

INGREDIENTS	METHOD
¼ cup margarine	*Cream.*
½ cup brown sugar	*Add gradually to margarine and cream well.*
2 eggs, beaten ⅓ cup brandy	*Stir in.*
1½ tsps. baking soda 2 tblsps. milk	*Dissolve soda in milk and add alternately with sifted dry ingredients.*
1½ cups all-purpose flour ½ tsp. ground cloves ½ tsp. powdered allspice ½ tsp. grated nutmeg	*Sift together. Add about ¾ cup to above mixture. Mix other ¾ cup with nuts and fruits.*
3 cups coarsely chopped nuts 1 cup sliced candied cherries 1 cup washed and drained seedless raisins ½ cup finely sliced citron ½ cup finely sliced candied pineapple	*Add floured nuts and fruits to mixed batter and blend well.*

SPECIAL INSTRUCTIONS: Drop by teaspoon onto greased and floured cookie pans. Bake.

Oven Temperature: 250 degrees Fahrenheit.

Baking Time: 20 to 25 minutes, or until light brown in color.

Makes 8 to 10 dozen.

FIG COOKIES

INGREDIENTS	METHOD
1 cup butter	*Cream.*
¼ cup sugar 1 cup chopped pecans 1 tsp. vanilla	*Add sugar to butter and beat until fluffy.* *Stir in.*
2 cups all-purpose flour 1 cup soaked, drained and ground figs	*Sift flour, mix with figs and stir into above. Combine well.*

SPECIAL INSTRUCTIONS: Form the dough into small finger shapes, arrange on buttered cookie pans. Bake.

Oven Temperature: 300 degrees Fahrenheit.

Baking Time: 25 to 30 minutes, or until done.

Makes 5 dozen or more.

FIG-FILLED COOKIES

INGREDIENTS	METHOD
½ cup shortening ½ cup butter ½ cup sugar	*Cream together well.*
½ cup honey 2 eggs, beaten	*Beat in. Mix well.*
4½ cups all-purpose flour 1 tsp. baking powder ½ tsp. salt	*Sift together and add to egg mixture gradually, beating well after each addition.*
Fig Filling (See page 288)	*See instructions below.*

SPECIAL INSTRUCTIONS: Place dough in refrigerator until well chilled. Roll out into 2 long strips, spread 1 strip with Fig Filling (Page 288) or jam and cover with the other dough strip. Pinch together. Bake.

Oven Temperature: 400 degrees Fahrenheit.

Baking Time: 8 to 10 minutes, or until delicately browned around the edges.

When cool, cut into oblong cookies.

Or shape the unbaked dough into 2 rolls, each about 2 inches in diameter. Wrap in waxed paper and chill in refrigerator for several hours. To bake, slice thin and put together in pairs, sandwich fashion, with a dot of commercial or home-made Fig Filling or jam between them. Press edges together lightly. Prick top with a fork. Bake as described.

Makes about 5 or 6 dozen cookies.

FIG PILLOWS

INGREDIENTS	METHOD
1½ cups all-purpose flour ⅛ tsp. salt	*Sift together into a mixing bowl.*
1 cup butter (room temperature) 1 cup soft cream cheese (8-oz. package) ½ tsp. vanilla	*Cut butter into flour until all is fine crumbs. Combine with cheese and vanilla until well blended and it forms a dough you can roll out.*
Fig Filling (See page 288)	*See instructions below.*

SPECIAL INSTRUCTIONS: Roll dough out on well floured board. Cut with a 2 or 3-inch round cookie cutter. Place about ⅔ teaspoon Fig Filling (Page 288) in center of each cookie and fold over. Seal the edges by pressing with prongs of fork. Bake.

Oven Temperature: 350 degrees Fahrenheit.

Baking Time: 10 to 12 minutes, or until cookies are lightly browned.

Makes almost 4 dozen cookies.

Fig-Filled Cookies

FIG CIRCLES

INGREDIENTS	METHOD
½ cup butter or margarine	*Cream.*
1 cup granulated sugar	*Add sugar and cream together thoroughly.*
1 egg 1 tsp. vanilla 3 tblsps. cream	*Beat egg and add with vanilla and cream.*
2¾ cups all-purpose flour ½ tsp. salt 1½ tsps. baking powder	*Sift together and add to egg-sugar mixture.*
Special Fig Filling (See page 287)	*See instructions below.*

SPECIAL INSTRUCTIONS: Chill dough thoroughly. Roll out ¼ inch thick. Cut half the dough in rounds, the remainder in doughnut shapes of the same size. Spread rounds with Special Fig Filling (Page 287). Top each round with doughnut ring. Press together gently. Place on cookie pan. Bake.

Oven Temperature: 375 degrees Fahrenheit.

Baking Time: 12 to 15 minutes.

When cool, sprinkle with confectioners' sugar.

Makes about 18 double cookies.

PINEAPPLE JAMBOREES

INGREDIENTS	METHOD
1¼ cups butter or margarine	*Cream.*
1 cup granulated sugar	*Add gradually, cream until light.*
2 eggs 2 tsps. vanilla	*Add and beat well.*
3 cups all-purpose flour ½ tsp. salt	*Sift flour and salt together and add gradually. Mix thoroughly.*
Pineapple preserves	*See instructions below.*

SPECIAL INSTRUCTIONS: Press through the star-plate of the cookie press, or use a star tube and a pastry bag. Form cookies in circles on ungreased cookie pans. Do not leave an opening in the center, but make a depression after the cookie has been shaped. Fill depression with ¼ teaspoon pineapple preserves. Bake.

Oven Temperature: 375 degrees Fahrenheit.

Baking Time: 10 to 12 minutes.

NOTE: This dough may be dropped from a teaspoon and an indentation made in each with spoon or finger.

Makes about 32 cookies.

HEALTH RAISIN COOKIES

INGREDIENTS	METHOD
1 cup water 2 cups washed and drained seedless raisins	*Boil together 5 minutes, or until liquid has decreased to ½ cup. Let cool.*
1 cup shortening	*Cream.*
2 cups sugar	*Add to shortening and blend well.*
3 eggs	*Add 1 at a time, beating well after each addition.*
1 tsp. vanilla 1 cup chopped nuts	*Add together with the cooled raisin mixture.*
4 cups all-purpose flour 1 tsp. baking powder 1 tsp. baking soda 2 tsps. salt 1½ tsps. powdered cinnamon ¼ tsp. powdered allspice	*Sift together flour and dry ingredients, add to the egg mixture gradually, beating after each addition. If additional liquid is needed add another beaten egg mixed with a little milk.*

SPECIAL INSTRUCTIONS: Drop by teaspoon onto greased cookie pans. Bake.

Oven Temperature: 400 degrees Fahrenheit.

Baking Time: 12 to 15 minutes.

Makes 9 or 10 dozen drop cookies.

HOLLAND DUTCH COOKIES

INGREDIENTS	METHOD
4 tblsps. butter 3 tblsps. granulated sugar 1 egg	*Mix butter and sugar together until smooth and creamy. Beat egg and mix in.*
⅓ cup molasses ¼ cup buttermilk ½ cup ground pecans	*Add to egg mixture and beat until well blended.*
1¾ cups all-purpose flour 1½ tsps. baking soda ¼ tsp. salt 1 tsp. powdered cinnamon ¼ tsp. ground mace ¼ tsp. ground cloves	*Sift all dry ingredients together and add to buttermilk combination.*
¼ cup mixed candied fruit	*Cut fine, add and incorporate well into the dough.*

SPECIAL INSTRUCTIONS: Spoon dough into a small, deep, square pan lined with waxed paper. Place in refrigerator for about 4 hours, or as long as overnight. Remove dough from pan, cut into square bars and then into ¼-inch thick cookies. Place on lightly greased cookie pans and bake.

Oven Temperature: 375 degrees Fahrenheit.

Baking Time: 12 to 15 minutes.

Makes about 48 or more.

WHEAT-FLAKE JUMBLES

INGREDIENTS	METHOD
⅓ cup shortening	*Cream.*
½ cup light brown sugar	*Add gradually to shortening and blend.*
1 egg, well beaten 1½ tblsps. milk	*Add and mix.*
1 cup all-purpose flour ½ tsp. baking powder ¼ tsp. baking soda ½ tsp. salt	*Sift together. Stir into creamed mixture.*
½ tsp. vanilla ½ cup pitted and finely cut dates ½ cup chopped walnuts	*Add to combined mixtures.*
1½ cups whole-wheat flakes	*Crush slightly.*

SPECIAL INSTRUCTIONS: Drop cookie dough from teaspoon into crushed wheat flakes and with spoon roll dough to completely coat it. Decorate top of each with nut half if desired. Place about 3 inches apart on heavily greased pans. Bake.

Oven Temperature: 375 degrees Fahrenheit.

Baking Time: about 15 minutes.

Makes 48 or more cookies.

MINCEMEAT COOKIES

INGREDIENTS	METHOD
¼ cup shortening	*Cream.*
½ cup granulated sugar	*Add gradually to short-ening and cream together until light.*
1 egg, beaten	*Add to sugar mixture and mix well.*
1½ cups all-purpose flour 1½ tsps. baking powder	*Sift together.*
1 cup mincemeat	*Add alternately with flour mixture to egg combination. Mix well.*

SPECIAL INSTRUCTIONS: Drop mixture by teaspoon onto a greased and floured pan. Bake.

Oven Temperature: 350 degrees Fahrenheit.

Baking Time: 10 to 12 minutes.

Makes about 60 or more drop cookies.

MINCEMEAT NUGGETS

INGREDIENTS	METHOD
1 cup butter 2 cups granulated sugar	*Cream together well.*
3 eggs, beaten	*Beat, add and mix well.*
4 cups all-purpose flour 1 tsp. baking soda ⅛ tsp. ground ginger ½ tsp. ground cloves ½ tsp. grated nutmeg ½ tsp. salt	*Sift together and add alternately with mincemeat and nuts to egg mixture.*
¾ cup mincemeat ½ cup chopped walnuts	

SPECIAL INSTRUCTIONS: Drop mixture from a teaspoon onto greased cookie pans, about 2 inches apart. Bake.
Oven Temperature: 375 degrees Fahrenheit.
Baking Time: about 12 minutes.
Makes 15 dozen or more.

*Raisin-Pecan
Crunch Delights*

RAISIN-PECAN CRUNCH DELIGHTS

INGREDIENTS	METHOD
1 cup margarine	*Cream.*
¾ cup granulated sugar ½ cup light brown sugar	*Add to margarine gradually and cream well.*
1 egg 1 tsp. vanilla ½ tsp. almond extract	*Beat egg, add with flavorings and blend in.*
1½ cups broken Pecan Crunch ½ cup washed and drained seedless raisins	*Crush the Crunch and add with raisins to egg combination.*
2¼ cups all-purpose flour ½ tsp. cream of tartar ½ tsp. baking soda	*Sift together, add to above and mix well together.*

SPECIAL INSTRUCTIONS: Drop mixture by teaspoon onto greased cookie pans. Bake.

Oven Temperature: 360 degrees Fahrenheit.

Baking Time: about 12 minutes.

Makes about 100 cookies.

RAISIN JUMBLES

INGREDIENTS	METHOD
½ cup margarine 1 cup brown sugar	*Cream together until light.*
1 egg	*Add and mix well.*
½ cup commercial sour cream	*Blend in.*
1⅔ cups all-purpose flour ¼ tsp. baking soda 1 tsp. baking powder ½ tsp. salt ¼ tsp. powdered cinnamon	*Sift together, add to creamed mixture, mix until well blended.*
½ cup pecan pieces ½ cup washed and drained seedless raisins	*Combine and add to the above, mix until evenly combined.*

SPECIAL INSTRUCTIONS: Drop dough by teaspoon 2 inches apart, onto greased and floured cookie pans. Bake.

Oven Temperature: 350 degrees Fahrenheit.

Baking Time: 12 to 15 minutes.

Sift confectioners' sugar over cookies when cool.

Makes about 30 to 40 jumbles.

RAISIN HERMITS

INGREDIENTS	METHOD
¾ cup butter (at room temperature) 1½ cups brown sugar	*Cream until light and fluffy.*
2 eggs	*Add 1 at a time, cream well.*
2 cups all-purpose flour 1 tsp. ground cloves 1 tsp. powdered cinnamon ¾ tsp. salt 1 tsp. baking soda	*Sift together, add ½ of flour mixture to the creamed mixture.*
2 tblsps. hot water	*Add remaining flour mixture alternately with hot water.*
1 cup seedless raisins, washed, drained and chopped ½ cup chopped pecans	*Fold in, mix thoroughly.*

SPECIAL INSTRUCTIONS: Drop by teaspoon onto well greased and floured cookie pans. Bake.

Oven Temperature: 350 degrees Fahrenheit.

Baking Time: 10 to 12 minutes.

Makes 75 to 80 hermits.

NORWEGIAN CURRANT COOKIES

INGREDIENTS	METHOD
½ cup butter	*Cream.*
2 egg yolks	*Beat eggs and stir in.*
¼ cup granulated sugar	*Mix in.*
1 cup all-purpose flour ½ tsp. vanilla or lemon extract ½ tsp. orange extract	*Sift flour. Add to sugar-egg mixture. Stir in flavorings.*
1 cup washed and drained currants	*See instructions below.*

SPECIAL INSTRUCTIONS: Put dough through cookie press onto lightly floured cookie pans. Brush each with milk and sprinkle thickly with currants. Bake.

Oven Temperature: 375 degrees Fahrenheit.

Baking Time: about 10 minutes.

Makes 24 or more cookies.

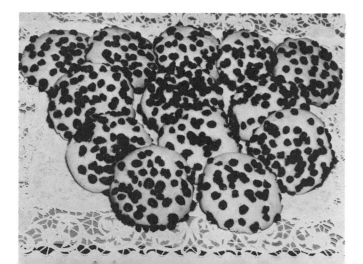

TUTTI-FRUTTI GEMS

INGREDIENTS	METHOD
1 cup margarine	*Melt slowly, let cool.*
1 cup molasses 1 egg	*Add to margarine and beat well.*
2 cups all-purpose flour 1½ tsps. baking soda 1 tsp. salt 1 tsp. powdered cinnamon 1 tsp. grated nutmeg	*Sift together and add to above.*
1 cup washed and drained seedless raisins 1 cup nuts ¾ cup candied citron, orange and lemon peels	*Put through fine blade of food chopper. Add to dough and mix thoroughly.*

SPECIAL INSTRUCTIONS: Drop by teaspoon onto well greased and floured cookie pans. Bake.

Oven Temperature: 425 degrees Fahrenheit.

Baking Time: 8 to 10 minutes until brown.

Makes about 96 cookies.

RASPBERRY-JAM DATERS

INGREDIENTS	METHOD
2½ cups all-purpose flour 1 tsp. salt	*Sift into a large mixing bowl.*
1 cup butter	*Cut in until particles are fine.*
6 to 8 tblsps. cold water	*Sprinkle over mixture, stir with fork until dough is moist enough to hold together.*
Raspberry jam or Date-Nut Filling (See page 310)	*See instructions below.*

SPECIAL INSTRUCTIONS: Roll out ½ of dough on floured surface ⅛ inch thick. Cut 36 cookies, using 2½-inch round cookie cutter. Transfer to ungreased cookie pans. Place 1 teaspoon raspberry jam or Date-Nut Filling (Page 310) in center of each cookie. Moisten edges. Roll out remaining dough and cut 36 cookies with 2½-inch doughnut cutter. Place these rings on top of cookies on cookie pans. Press edges together to seal. Brush top with milk and sprinkle with granulated sugar. Bake.

Oven Temperature: 400 degrees Fahrenheit.

Baking Time: 12 to 15 minutes.

Makes 36 double cookies.

SOUR-CREAM DROPS

INGREDIENTS	METHOD
½ cup margarine ¾ cup granulated sugar ¼ tsp. salt	*Cream together.*
1 egg ½ tsp. lemon extract	*Beat egg, add with flavoring to creamed butter-sugar mixture.*
1½ cups Fig Filling (See page 288) ½ cup commercial sour cream	*Stir in.*
1½ cups all-purpose flour ½ tsp. baking soda ¼ tsp. baking powder ¼ tsp. powdered cinnamon ¼ tsp. grated nutmeg	*Sift together, add to sour cream mixture and blend thoroughly.*
Pecan or walnut halves	*See instructions below.*

SPECIAL INSTRUCTIONS: Drop mixture onto greased cookie pans. Top each rounded teaspoon of dough with a pecan or walnut half. Bake.

Oven Temperature: 375 to 400 degrees Fahrenheit.

Baking Time: 10 to 12 minutes.

Makes about 96 cookies.

FRUITED DROP COOKIES

INGREDIENTS	METHOD
1½ cups seedless raisins 1½ cups currants	*Wash and drain.*
1½ cups candied pine- apple 1½ cups candied cherries ½ cup citron, sliced thin 1½ cups broken nuts	*Cut or chop fruit and nuts into very small pieces.*
½ cup shortening	*Cream until smooth.*
1½ cups brown sugar	*Add gradually to short- ening, cream until well blended.*
3 egg yolks	*Beat and mix into sugar combination.*
1½ tsps. vinegar ½ cup evaporated milk	*Mix together and add to creamed mixture alter- nating with some of the sifted dry ingredients. Combine smoothly.*

2 cups all-purpose flour ½ tsp. baking soda ½ tsp. salt 1 tsp. powdered cinnamon 1 tsp. ground cloves 1 tsp. powdered allspice Dash grated nutmeg	*Add rest of sifted flour, soda, salt and spices to the fruits and nuts. Blend into sugar-egg mixture.*
3 egg whites	*Whip until stiff but not dry. Fold into batter.*

SPECIAL INSTRUCTIONS: Drop by teaspoon onto greased and floured cookie pans. Bake.

Oven Temperature: 300 degrees Fahrenheit.

Baking Time: 20 to 25 minutes.

Makes 10 dozen or more.

POLKA-DOT COOKIES

INGREDIENTS	METHOD
1 cup butter 2 cups sugar 1 tsp. vanilla	*Cream butter, add sugar and vanilla and continue creaming until well mixed.*
3 eggs	*Beat well and add to butter mixture. Blend well.*
4 cups all-purpose flour ½ tsp. salt	*Sift together, add to mixture using a little more flour if necessary, to make a stiff dough.*
Raspberry jam	*See instructions below.*

SPECIAL INSTRUCTIONS: Chill 20 to 30 minutes, or overnight. Roll out to ⅛-inch thickness. Cut ½ of the dough with 2-inch plain or fluted cookie cutter. Cut the remaining dough with a doughnut cutter. Place on cookie pans. Bake.

Oven Temperature: 400 degrees Fahrenheit.

Baking Time: about 10 minutes.

Let cool. Then put a dab of raspberry jam on each bottom cookie and set a cut-out ring on top, pressing together gently. Sift confectioners' sugar over tops.

Makes about 40 filled cookies.

9. GINGER AND MOLASSES COOKIES

GINGER DELIGHTS

INGREDIENTS	METHOD
½ cup butter 1 cup granulated sugar	*Cream together until light and fluffy.*
2 eggs	*Beat eggs, add and mix well.*
1 tsp. baking soda 1 tblsp. water	*Combine and add to creamed mixture.*
1 cup molasses	*Blend in.*
4 cups all-purpose flour 1 tsp. ground ginger	*Sift together, gradually add to molasses mixture and blend well.*

SPECIAL INSTRUCTIONS: Drop by teaspoon onto greased and lightly floured cookie pans and bake.
Oven Temperature: 350 degrees Fahrenheit.
Baking Time: 12 to 15 minutes.
Let cool. Frost with Confectioners' Icing (Page 295).
Makes about 100 cookies.

DARK MOLASSES COOKIES

INGREDIENTS	METHOD
1 cup shortening 1 cup brown sugar	*Cream together.*
2 eggs	*Beat eggs, add and blend well.*
1 cup molasses	*Add to above and blend.*
4 cups all-purpose flour 3 tsps. baking soda 3 tsps. powdered cinnamon 3 tsps. ground ginger 1 tsp. grated nutmeg	*Sift together, add to molasses mixture, blend thoroughly.*
1 cup all-bran cereal 1 cup chopped walnuts 1 cup washed and drained seedless raisins	*Mix into dough and blend evenly.*
Granulated sugar	*See instructions.*

SPECIAL INSTRUCTIONS: Chill dough about ½ hour. Form into rolls about 1 inch in diameter. Wrap in waxed paper and chill for several hours. Cut off ¾-inch pieces and roll in the fingers to form small balls. Dip each into granulated sugar and place sugared side up on greased and lightly floured cookie pans. Flatten each ball gently with the bottom of a glass. Bake.

Oven Temperature: 375 degrees Fahrenheit.

Baking Time: 12 to 14 minutes.

Makes 78 or more cookies.

OLD-FASHIONED SOFT GINGER COOKIES

INGREDIENTS	METHOD
¾ cup shortening 2 cups brown sugar	*Cream together thoroughly.*
⅔ cup molasses ⅔ cup boiling water	*Combine molasses and water and mix into creamed shortening.*
1 tblsp. ground ginger 2 tsps. baking soda 1 tsp. salt 4 cups all-purpose flour	*Sift together. Add to above, mix to a medium soft dough.*

SPECIAL INSTRUCTIONS: Pat and roll out to about ¼ inch thick. Cut with a medium large cookie cutter. Place on greased and lightly floured cookie pans and bake.

Oven Temperature: 325 degrees Fahrenheit.

Baking Time: 20 to 25 minutes.

Let cool. Leave plain or ice and decorate with a medium stiff Confectioners' Icing (Page 295).

Makes 48 or more cookies.

ROUND GINGER SNAPS

INGREDIENTS	METHOD
½ cup margarine ½ cup light brown sugar	*Cream together for about 5 minutes.*
⅓ cup milk 1 tsp. instant coffee powder ⅓ cup molasses	*Mix milk, coffee powder and molasses together. Beat into creamed mixture.*
2½ cups all-purpose flour, or enough to make soft dough ½ tsp. salt ½ tsp. baking soda ½ tsp. ground allspice ½ tsp. ground ginger ¼ tsp. ground cloves ½ tsp. powdered cinnamon	*Sift together and add to molasses mixture gradually. Blend well.*

SPECIAL INSTRUCTIONS: Place dough in refrigerator long enough to chill through. Roll it very thin, no more than ⅛ inch thick, on a floured cloth. Cut with a 2-inch cookie cutter. Bake.

Oven Temperature: 350 degrees Fahrenheit.

Baking Time: about 15 minutes.

Let cool. Leave plain or decorate with White Icing Glaze (Page 300).

Makes 30 or more cookies.

BLACK-MAGIC COOKIES

INGREDIENTS	METHOD
½ cup shortening ⅓ cup brown sugar	*Cream together until light and fluffy.*
1 egg ½ cup molasses ¼ cup coffee, milk or water	*Beat egg, add with molasses and other liquid and blend well.*
2 cups all-purpose flour ½ tsp. salt ½ tsp. ground ginger or cloves ½ tsp. powdered cinnamon 1 tsp. baking soda	*Sift all together, add to egg mixture and beat well.*

SPECIAL INSTRUCTIONS: Crisp cookies can be made by keeping the mixture as thin as possible. A little more flour added will make the cookies thicker and softer, but too much flour added makes hard and dry cookies. Place heaping teaspoons of dough on greased cookie pans. Bake.

Oven Temperature: 375 degrees Fahrenheit.

Baking Time: about 10 minutes.

NOTE: To vary these cookies, add ¼ teaspoon each of grated nutmeg and allspice to the dry ingredients. Or add ½ cup washed, drained and floured seedless raisins, using some of the flour in the recipe to coat them with.

Makes about 34 cookies.

COOKIE CIRCLES

INGREDIENTS	METHOD
½ cup butter or margarine 1 cup granulated sugar	*Cream together.*
1 egg ½ tsp. orange extract ¼ cup molasses ½ tsp. baking soda	*Beat egg; combine molasses, soda and vinegar and stir well. Add all with flavoring to butter-sugar mixture.*
2½ cups all-purpose flour ½ tsp. salt	*Sift together and carefully mix in until well blended.*

SPECIAL INSTRUCTIONS: Roll out on well floured cloth or board into ⅛-inch thickness. Cut out with a 2-inch fluted cookie cutter. Place on lightly greased and floured pans. Brush lightly with a mixture of 1 beaten egg, pinch of salt and 2 tablespoons milk. Or brush with milk. Place a half pecan, walnut or candied cherry in center of each cookie and bake.

Oven Temperature: 350 degrees Fahrenheit.

Baking Time: 8 to 10 minutes or until a golden brown.

Makes about 20 cookies.

10. HOLIDAY COOKIES

CHRISTMAS TREE COOKIES

INGREDIENTS	METHOD
1 cup shortening	*Cream thoroughly.*
¾ cup granulated sugar	*Add gradually to shortening beating smooth.*
1 egg	*Beat egg and add to sugar mixture.*
2¼ cups all-purpose flour ⅛ tsp. salt ¼ tsp. baking powder	*Sift together and add.*
1 tsp. almond extract Few drops green pure-food coloring	*Add to above and mix well.*

SPECIAL INSTRUCTIONS: Fill a cookie press, use the tree plate of the press, and form cookies on greased cookie pans. Decorate with mixed miniature colored candies. Bake.

Oven Temperature: 400 degrees Fahrenheit.

Baking Time: 10 to 12 minutes.

Makes about 30 tree cookies; more if tree plate is small.

COLORED-SUGAR CHRISTMAS TREES

INGREDIENTS	METHOD
4 tblsps. shortening 1½ cups granulated sugar 3 egg yolks 2 egg whites 1 tsp. lemon juice	*Cream sugar and shortening together until fluffy. Beat yolks and 2 whites with lemon juice and mix in well.*
2⅓ cups all-purpose flour 2½ tsps. baking powder 1¼ tsps. powdered cinnamon ¼ tsp. salt ¼ tsp. grated nutmeg	*Sift flour and dry ingredients. Blend into egg mixture.*
½ cup finely ground walnuts	*Stir walnuts into dough.*
1 egg white	*Beat until frothy.*

SPECIAL INSTRUCTIONS: Roll ⅛ of dough at a time, on lightly floured cloth-covered board to ⅛-inch thickness. Cut with Christmas-tree cutter. Brush cookies with the beaten egg white. Sprinkle with Colored Sugar (Page 305). Bake.

Oven Temperature: 375 degrees Fahrenheit.

Baking Time: 6 to 8 minutes.

Makes 2 dozen or more trees.

WREATHS

INGREDIENTS	METHOD
½ cup butter 2 egg yolks	*Cream together.*
½ cup granulated sugar	*Add gradually and continue creaming until light.*
1 cup all-purpose flour ½ tsp. grated orange rind ½ tsp. orange extract	*Stir flour in gradually, adding orange rind and flavoring.*

SPECIAL INSTRUCTIONS: Roll dough very thin onto a floured board. Cut wreaths with a floured doughnut or wreath cutter. Decorate each with bits of candied fruits or red and green sugars. Bake on unbuttered cookie pans.

Oven Temperature: 350 degrees Fahrenheit.

Baking Time: 8 to 10 minutes.

Let wreaths cool. If desired, dot them with silver dragees using very little corn syrup to affix them.

NOTE: Rum may be substituted for the orange extract as flavoring.

Makes 16 or more wreaths.

Colored-Sugar Christmas Trees

ANIMAL CUTOUTS

INGREDIENTS	METHOD
½ cup margarine or shortening	*Cream.*
1 cup granulated sugar	*Add gradually and cream until light.*
1 egg, well beaten 1 tsp. vanilla 1 tblsp. milk or cream	*Add to creamed mixture and blend in.*
1½ cups all-purpose flour 1½ tsps. baking powder ½ tsp. salt	*Sift together and add to creamed mixture.*
½ cup sifted all-purpose flour	*Add as needed to make dough stiff enough to handle.*

SPECIAL INSTRUCTIONS: Chill dough at least 1 hour. Roll ⅛ inch thick on lightly floured board. Cut with floured animal cookie cutters. Place on ungreased cookie pans and brush with a little water or mixture of 1 beaten egg, pinch of salt and 2 tablespoons milk. Sprinkle cookies with colored sugar. Or leave plain and frost after baking with icing. Page 305 for Colored Sugar recipe.

Oven Temperature: 375 degrees Fahrenheit.

Baking Time: 10 to 12 minutes.

Makes 40 or more small to medium animal cookies.

ANISE DROPS

INGREDIENTS	METHOD
4 eggs	*Beat until light.*
1½ cups granulated sugar	*Add slowly to eggs, continue beating until lemon colored.*
3 cups all-purpose flour ¾ tsp. baking powder ⅛ tsp. salt 2½ tsps. ground anise seeds	*Sift together, add gradually to egg mixture. Blend with wire whip.*

SPECIAL INSTRUCTIONS: Drop mixture from teaspoon, or use pastry bag and No. 6 plain tube, onto greased and floured cookie pans. Let stand uncovered in cool dry place overnight, or about 10 hours, to dry tops of cookies. Bake.

Oven Temperature: 350 degrees Fahrenheit.

Baking Time: 10 to 15 minutes.

NOTE: Bake only until a very light, delicate brown. Let cool. Place in an air-tight container to mellow.

Makes 40 or more cookies.

GINGERBREAD BOYS AND GIRLS

INGREDIENTS	METHOD
¼ cup boiling water ½ cup butter	*Pour water over butter. Stir to blend.*
½ cup brown sugar ½ cup dark molasses	*Add to butter and mix well.*
3 cups all-purpose flour 1 tsp. baking soda 1 tsp. salt 1½ tsps. ground ginger ½ tsp. grated nutmeg ⅛ tsp. ground cloves	*Sift together, add to above and blend well.*

SPECIAL INSTRUCTIONS: Chill dough thoroughly. Roll out on floured cloth to ⅛- or ¼-inch thickness. Cut with gingerbread boy and girl cutters. Place cookies on greased cookie pan. Bake.

Oven Temperature: 375 degrees Fahrenheit.

Baking Time: about 10 minutes.

NOTE: Gingerbread boy and girl pictures to stick on the cookies are available from pastry supply shops. Or decorate the cookies with colored icing.

Makes 1½ to 2 dozen small cookies.

GINGERBREAD MEN

INGREDIENTS	METHOD
½ cup molasses	*Heat to boiling point, remove from heat.*
¼ cup sugar 1½ tblsps. margarine 1½ tblsps. shortening 1 tblsp. milk	*Add to above and mix together.*
2 cups all-purpose flour ½ tsp. baking soda ½ tsp. salt ½ tsp. ground cloves ½ tsp. powdered cinnamon ½ tsp. grated nutmeg	*Sift together, add to above and mix well.*

SPECIAL INSTRUCTIONS: Chill dough. Roll out to about ⅛-inch thickness. Cut either with a knife or with a gingerbread man cookie cutter. Place on greased cookie pans. Bake.

Oven Temperature: 350 degrees Fahrenheit.

Baking Time: about 10 minutes.

Decorate gingerbread men with Confectioners' Icing (Page 295). Use raisins for eyes, miniature candies or dots of icing for smile. Pictures of Santa Claus and other figures are available from card shops and novelty stores. They can be stuck on cookies with Confectioners' Icing.

Makes about 24 gingerbread men.

GINGERBREAD HOUSES

INGREDIENTS	METHOD
1 cup shortening 1 cup light brown sugar ¾ cup molasses	*Mix together until smooth.*
½ cup hot water	*Stir into above and mix well.*
2 eggs	*Beat eggs and stir into the sugar mixture.*
5½ cups all-purpose flour 1 tsp. salt 2 tsps. baking soda 2 tsps. ground ginger 1 tsp. ground cloves 1 tsp. powdered cinnamon	*Sift together, add slowly, mixing so as to make a smooth dough.*

SPECIAL INSTRUCTIONS: Place dough on floured pan and chill. Toss dough on floured board or pastry cloth, roll to about ⅛- or ¼-inch thickness. Cut out with a pointed knife using cardboard patterns for the sides, front, roof, etc. of the gingerbread houses. Bake.

Oven Temperature: 375 degrees Fahrenheit.

Baking Time: 15 to 20 minutes.

Let cool. Put together into houses with a stiff Royal Icing (Page 297). Decorate with candies, small cookies, snow, icicles, as illustrated. Build each house on a platter.

Gingerbread House No. 1

At the left there is a crib with tiny infant doll and animals. A Santa Claus and pine trees decorate the right side. There are 2 small reindeer on the roof, and smoke coming from the chimney. Bits of iced cake dough outline the path.

Gingerbread House No. 2

This photograph shows a house with steps in front and walks leading into the street, steps are cookies. The walks are made with Royal Icing, the same icing which you use to put the sides of the house together. The snow man and lady, at right, are small tree decoration figures. The roof, as you can see, is decorated with Royal Icing to represent shingles or tiles. Santa coming out of the chimney on the left, is small toy ready to use.

BROWN LEBKUCHEN

INGREDIENTS	METHOD
½ cup honey 2 tblsps. corn syrup 1 cup brown sugar ¼ cup water ½ tsp. vanilla	*Combine and heat to boiling. Remove from heat.*
2 egg yolks, beaten	*Add and stir well.*
3¾ cups all-purpose flour ⅛ tsp. allspice ⅛ tsp. grated nutmeg ⅛ tsp. ground cloves ¼ tsp. powdered cinnamon ¼ tsp. baking soda	*Sift together and add, mixing to a smooth dough.*
3 tblsps. candied orange peel 3 tblsps. candied citron ½ cup finely chopped walnuts	*Cut or chop the fruit fine, add to dough with nuts, mix all in blender or knead until smooth.*

SPECIAL INSTRUCTIONS: Knead or beat dough well, using a little extra flour for dusting until you have a stiff dough. Place in bowl, cover with waxed paper or foil and let age in a cool place for at least 3 days. After 3 days, roll dough out ¼ inch thick, cut in rectangular pieces, 2 by 4 inches. Place on cookie pan, brush with 1 beaten egg mixed with two tablespoons milk and a pinch of salt. Decorate with chopped candied cherries and nuts or leave plain. Bake.

Oven Temperature: 350 degrees Fahrenheit.

Baking Time: 12 to 15 minutes.

Let cool. Frost with White Icing Glaze (Page 300).

Makes 36 or more lebkuchen.

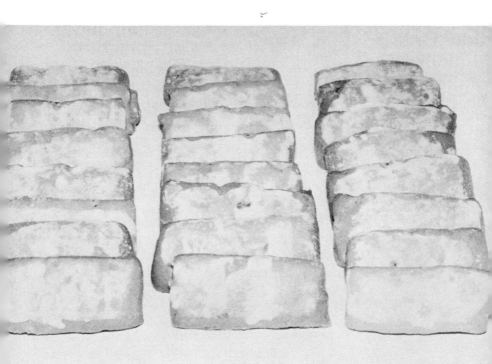

GINGER LEBKUCHEN

INGREDIENTS	METHOD
1½ cups all-purpose flour 1 tsp. baking powder ¼ tsp. baking soda ½ tsp. salt 2 tsps. ground ginger	*Sift together.*
1 cup brown sugar ¼ cup shortening ⅓ cup molasses ¼ cup buttermilk	*Cream sugar and shortening together, combine with molasses. Add sifted dry ingredients and buttermilk alternately to form dough.*

SPECIAL INSTRUCTIONS: Roll dough out on well floured cloth or board to ⅛-inch thickness. Cut in rectangular pieces. Brush with a mixture of 1 beaten egg, pinch of salt, and 2 tablespoons milk. Bake.

Oven Temperature: 350 degrees Fahrenheit.

Baking Time: 15 to 18 minutes.

Let cool. Frost with Sugar Glaze (Page 301).

Makes about 18 lebkuchen.

HOLIDAY CUTOUTS I

INGREDIENTS	METHOD
1 cup shortening, margarine or butter	*Cream until smooth.*
2 cups fine granulated sugar	*Add to butter and beat together.*
2 eggs	*Add eggs 1 at a time to sugar mixture, beat well.*
1 tsp. lemon extract	*Add to above and mix in.*
½ tsp. baking soda 1 cup commercial sour cream 5 cups all-purpose flour	*Combine soda and sour cream, add alternately with sifted flour to egg mixture. Combine smoothly.*

SPECIAL INSTRUCTIONS: Roll dough out ⅛ inch thick. Cut out with any shape or size cookie cutter, such as star, bell, tree. Place carefully on lightly greased cookie pan. Cookies may be brushed with milk to make decorations stay on. Use colored sugar, nuts, chocolate dots, coconut, seedless raisins, currants, candied fruits. Bake.

Oven Temperature: 375 to 400 degrees Fahrenheit.

Baking Time: 8 to 10 minutes or until light brown edges form around cookies.

Makes 70 to 100 cookies.

HOLIDAY CUTOUTS II

INGREDIENTS	METHOD
1¼ cups hot mashed potatoes ½ cup sugar ¾ cup corn syrup 1 cup butter or margarine	*Mash thoroughly.* *Cream sugar, syrup and fat together, beat into potatoes.*
1 cup all-purpose flour (more if needed) 2 tsps. baking powder 1 tsp. cinnamon or ground allspice ¼ tsp. ground cloves ½ tsp. grated nutmeg ½ tsp. salt	*Sift together. Combine until smooth with above mixture. Add sufficient flour to make smooth dough.*
½ cup washed and drained seedless raisins or currants ¼ cup finely chopped nuts	*Chop currants or raisins fine, add with nuts to dough and mix well.*
1 egg	*See instructions below.*

SPECIAL INSTRUCTIONS: To make shamrock cookies for St. Patrick's Day, use a shamrock cutter or use a measuring spoon teaspoon-size and for each cookie drop 3 mounds of dough close together on lightly greased cookie pans. Arrange a bit of dough for the stem. Brush with slightly beaten egg and sprinkle with green sugar. For other holiday cookies, chill dough in refrigerator. Roll out and cut with appropriate cookie cutters, such as heart for Valentine's Day, bunnies for Easter, bell, tree, wreath for Christmas, etc.

Oven Temperature: 375 degrees Fahrenheit.

Baking Time: about 20 minutes.

Makes 40 or more cookies.

HOLIDAY CUTOUTS III

INGREDIENTS	METHOD
2 cups granulated sugar ½ cup margarine ½ cup shortening 1 tsp. salt	*Cream all together until smooth.*
2 eggs	*Beat and add to creamed mixture.*
1 cup milk 1 tsp. almond extract 1 tsp. vanilla	*Add alternately with sifted flour and baking powder to the egg mixture.*
5 cups all-purpose flour 4 tsps. baking powder	*Mix to a smooth dough.*

SPECIAL INSTRUCTIONS: Put dough in refrigerator ½ hour, or until cold enough to handle easily. Roll out on a well floured pastry cloth to ⅛-inch thickness. Use any holiday cookie cutter and cut out into cookies. Brush with a mixture of beaten egg, pinch of salt, and 2 tablespoons milk. Sprinkle with colored sugar, or finely ground nuts, chocolate shreds, coconut, etc. Bake on lightly greased cookie pans.

Oven Temperature: 350 degrees Fahrenheit.

Baking Time: 12 to 15 minutes.

NOTE: Cookies can also be baked plain. Let cool and decorate with white or colored icings (Page 295), or Chocolate Icing (Page 292).

Makes 70 to 100 cookies.

LOG COOKIES

INGREDIENTS	METHOD
½ cup butter ½ cup shortening ¾ cup granulated sugar	*Cream together until light and fluffy.*
1 egg 1 tsp. lemon extract 1 tsp. vanilla 1 tsp. almond extract	*Beat egg, combine with sugar mixture. Stir in flavorings.*
3 cups all-purpose flour	*Sift, add to egg mixture and mix until a smooth dough.*

SPECIAL INSTRUCTIONS: Cut dough in half. Roll out each half lightly, then shape it into a long thin (¾-inch thick) roll. Cut with sharp knife into 2-inch-long individual rolls. Place on lightly greased cookie pans. Bake.

Oven Temperature: 350 degrees Fahrenheit.

Baking Time: 10 to 12 minutes.

When baked, dip cookies into a white or chocolate icing (Page 292). Go over the icing, while it is still wet, with the tines of a fork so it will resemble the bark of a log. Sprinkle with fine coconut colored with a little green pure-food coloring.

Makes 36 to 40 or more logs.

PEPPERNUTS

INGREDIENTS	METHOD
4 cups all-purpose flour 1 tsp. baking soda ½ tsp. salt 1 tblsp. powdered cinnamon 1 tsp. ground cloves 1 tsp. grated nutmeg ¼ tsp. black pepper	*Combine and sift together into large bowl.*
1½ tsps. grated lemon rind 1 tblsp. crushed cardamom seeds 1 tsp. anise seeds	*Stir into the flour mixture.*
¼ lb. candied orange peel ½ lb. citron	*Grind both and then add to flour mixture. Use wooden spoon.*
2 tblsps. butter 2½ cups confectioners' sugar	*Cream together. Combine with flour-fruit mixture.*
5 eggs, well beaten ¼ cup milk or water	*Add eggs to flour mixture. Gradually stir in the milk or water. Blend all together.*
Confectioners' sugar	*See instructions below.*

SPECIAL INSTRUCTIONS: Chill 1 hour. Shape dough in small balls the size of a walnut. Place on floured cloth and let stand, uncovered, overnight at room temperature. Place on ungreased cookie pans. Bake.

Oven Temperature: 350 degrees Fahrenheit.

Baking Time: 15 to 20 minutes.

After baking, while cookies are still warm, roll them in confectioners' sugar. Repeat this when the cookies are cold.

Makes 80 or more peppernuts.

PEPPERNUT BUTTONS

INGREDIENTS	METHOD
½ cup granulated sugar ½ cup brown sugar 2 eggs	*Beat together until thick.*
½ cup finely chopped citron 1 tsp. grated orange rind 1 tsp. grated lemon rind	*Add to above, mix.*
1¾ cups all-purpose flour 1 tsp. baking powder 1 tsp. grated nutmeg ¼ tsp. ground cloves	*Sift together, add and mix well.*

SPECIAL INSTRUCTIONS: Roll dough into long roll, ¾ inch thick. Cut in ½-inch pieces. Bake on greased cookie pans.

Oven Temperature: 350 degrees Fahrenheit.

Baking Time: 12 to 15 minutes.

When baked and cooled lay cookies on pan or waxed paper and sprinkle with syrup made of 1 cup sugar and ¾ cup water boiled to 230 degrees Fahrenheit or soft-thread stage. Immediately sift confectioners' sugar over the coated cookies and turn them with 2 wooden spoons over and over until well coated. Let stand several hours. If colored Peppernut Buttons are desired, add a little pure-food coloring to the syrup before sprinkling it on the cookies.

Makes about 30 cookies.

WHITE PEPPERNUTS

INGREDIENTS	METHOD
3 cups all-purpose flour 1 tsp. baking powder ¾ tsp. salt $\frac{1}{16}$ tsp. black or white pepper 1 tsp. powdered cinnamon ½ tsp. ground mace 1 tsp. ground allspice	*Sift all together into a large mixing bowl.*
½ cup candied citron ¼ cup candied orange peel 1 tsp. grated fresh lemon rind	*Chop fruits fine, add to above.*
3 eggs 1½ cups granulated sugar	*Beat with sugar until thick and lemon colored. Add to first mixture and blend thoroughly. Knead with hands if necessary.*

SPECIAL INSTRUCTIONS: Pinch off small pieces of the dough about the size of a pecan. Shape into balls. Bake on greased cookie pans.

Oven Temperature: 350 degrees Fahrenheit.

Baking Time: 15 to 18 minutes, until a delicate brown.

Let cool. Store in air-tight container to ripen. Roll in confectioners' sugar before serving.

Makes about 9 to 10 dozen.

GERMAN SPRINGERLE

INGREDIENTS	METHOD
2 eggs ¼ cup fine granulated sugar	*Beat together until thick.*
1 cup fine granulated sugar	*Add gradually and beat well.*
2½ cups all-purpose flour ½ tsp. baking powder OR ¼ tsp. bakers' ammonia (powdered) ½ tsp. salt	*Sift together.*
1 tsp. crushed anise seeds 1 tsp. grated lemon rind	*Mix with the sifted ingredients. Beat into the egg mixture to make a medium stiff dough.*

SPECIAL INSTRUCTIONS: Roll dough on a well floured board to about ½-inch thickness. Dust lightly with flour. Press a springerle rolling pin over the dough to make the springerle designs. Cut the cookies in squares. Place them on a lightly greased cookie pan and let dry uncovered for at least 12 hours. Bake.

Oven Temperature: 325 degrees Fahrenheit.

Baking Time: 25 to 30 minutes. Bake very light.

Makes 50 or more cookies.

SPRINGERLE PICTURE COOKIES

INGREDIENTS	METHOD
1 egg yolk 3 eggs 1 cup granulated sugar	*Beat yolk, eggs and sugar together until very light.*
1 cup granulated sugar	*Add to above and beat 10 to 12 minutes longer or use blender 2 or 3 minutes.*
2½ cups all-purpose flour ½ tsp. salt ¾ tsp. baking powder 1 tsp. grated fresh lemon rind	*Sift flour, salt, and baking powder together. Add with lemon rind to sugar mixture and mix well.*
2 tblsps. anise seeds	*Use as described in instructions below.*

SPECIAL INSTRUCTIONS: With a regular rolling pin roll out dough on a well floured cloth to about ½-inch thickness. Then use a springerle rolling pin, or picture board, to make designs on the dough. Sprinkle cookie pan with 2 tablespoons anise seeds. Cut decorated dough into cookies, place on anise seed in pan. Let dry at least 8 to 10 hours, or overnight. Bake very light.

Oven Temperature: 325 degrees Fahrenheit.

Baking Time: 18 to 20 minutes.

NOTE: Springerle cookies are very hard German Christmas cookies. If placed in a covered canister or cookie jar they will soften and mellow into a delicious texture.

Makes 50 or more cookies.

HALLOWEEN COOKIES

INGREDIENTS	METHOD
½ cup shortening	*Cream.*
1 cup sugar	*Add gradually, beat until light.*
1 egg, beaten	*Add to sugar mixture.*
1 tsp. vanilla 2 tblsps. water	*Stir in.*
2 cups all-purpose flour ⅓ cup nonfat dry milk powder 1 tsp. baking powder ¾ tsp. salt	*Sift together, add gradually to egg mixture and combine well.*
2 oz. (squares) unsweetened chocolate	*Melt over hot water, let cool, add to above. Mix.*

SPECIAL INSTRUCTIONS: Divide dough into 3 portions. Wrap in waxed paper and chill several hours. Roll ⅔ of dough out ⅛ inch thick on lightly floured board. Use a witch-hat cookie cutter, or make a cardboard pattern in witch-hat shape. Cut round cookies from ⅓ of dough. Place on well greased cookie pans. Bake.

Oven Temperature: 400 degrees Fahrenheit.

Baking Time: 5 to 8 minutes.

Decorate cooled cookies with cats, pumpkin-faces, and children's names, using Confectioners' Icing (Page 295) or Royal Icing (Page 297).

Makes about 36 cookies.

NEW YEAR'S COOKIES

INGREDIENTS	METHOD
1¼ cups fine, granulated sugar ½ cup margarine ½ cup shortening	*Cream together until smooth.*
1 egg, beaten 1 tblsp. milk ¼ cup light corn syrup ½ tsp. baking soda	*Combine and mix well, add to sugar mixture alternately with sifted flour mixture.*
3 cups all-purpose flour 1 tsp. ground ginger ½ tsp. salt ½ tsp. cocoa powder	*Sift together, add as described above, and mix until smooth.*

SPECIAL INSTRUCTIONS: Roll dough out to ⅛-inch thickness. Cut with a 2½-inch round, fluted cookie cutter and brush lightly with milk. Fill center with a dot of thick fruit jam or any preferred filling which will not run when baked. Fold opposite sides over the filling, barely overlapping. Bake.

Oven Temperature: 350 degrees Fahrenheit.

Baking Time: about 15 minutes.

VARIATION: Use bell-shaped cookie cutter. Do not fold over. Sprinkle with a little colored sugar. Bake as described.

Makes about 36 cookies.

11. HONEY COOKIES

BASIC HONEY COOKIES

INGREDIENTS	METHOD
½ cup honey 1 egg 3 or 4 tblsps. milk (variable) 3 tblsps. butter 1 tblsp. grated lemon rind 2 tblsps. grated orange rind	*Beat egg, combine with milk, honey and butter. Add rinds.*
4 cups all-purpose flour (or less) 1 tsp. powdered cinnamon 1 tsp. baking soda ½ tsp. ground cloves ½ tsp. grated nutmeg ¼ tsp. ground allspice ¼ tsp. ground mace	*Sift together, combine with above mixture.*

*A Fancy Sugar
Barrel of
Assorted
Cookies*

3 tblsps. chopped citron
3 tblsps. candied lemon
   peel
2 tblsps. candied orange
   peel
	Chop all fine, work into dough.

SPECIAL INSTRUCTIONS: Roll out the dough ¼ inch thick on lightly floured board. Cut out bells, stars, diamonds, and other designs with floured cookie cutters. Transfer to buttered cookie pans. Brush top of cookies with a mixture of 1 beaten egg, pinch of salt, and 2 tablespoons milk. Decorate with an almond or candied cherry, or a few seedless raisins. Bake.

Oven Temperature: 350 degrees Fahrenheit.

Baking Time: 8 to 10 minutes until they are a light brown.

Makes 50 or more cookies.

NUERNBERGER LEBKUCHEN

INGREDIENTS	METHOD
1 cup honey	*Heat to boiling in sauce-pan, remove from heat and let cool.*
¾ cup brown sugar 1 egg 1 tblsp. lemon juice 1 tsp. grated lemon rind	*Beat egg, combine with sugar. Stir into honey with lemon juice and rind.*
2¾ cups all-purpose flour 1½ tsps. baking soda 1 tsp. powdered cinnamon 1 tsp. ground allspice ½ tsp. grated nutmeg ¼ tsp. ground cloves	*Sift together, stir into honey mixture.*
⅓ cup finely chopped citron ⅓ cup finely chopped nuts	*Stir into dough.*

SPECIAL INSTRUCTIONS: Chill dough overnight in refrigerator. Roll small amount of dough; keep rest chilled. Roll out ¼ inch thick; cut into 2-inch squares or rounds. Brush with mixture of 1 egg, pinch of salt and 2 tablespoons milk. Decorate with candied fruit and nuts. Place on greased cookie pans. Bake.

Oven Temperature: 390 degrees Fahrenheit.

Baking Time: 10 to 12 minutes, or until set.

Immediately brush with White Icing Glaze (Page 300). Remove from cookie pan. Let cool and mellow.

Makes 90 or more cookies.

NUERNBERGER HONEY COOKIES

INGREDIENTS	METHOD
4 eggs ¾ cup chopped, mixed candied fruit 1 tsp. grated lemon rind ¾ cup blanched, chopped almonds 2 tblsps. powdered cinnamon 1 tsp. ground cloves 1 tsp. salt 2½ cups confectioners' sugar 1½ cups honey 2 tblsps. orange juice OR 2 tblsps. rum flavoring	*Beat eggs until thick and light in large bowl. Add fruits, nuts, spice, salt and mix well. Add sugar and honey with flavoring to egg mixture.*
2 tsps. baking soda 1 tblsp. hot water	*Stir soda into water and add.*
4 cups all-purpose flour	*Sift and add to above gradually. Mix until smooth.*

SPECIAL INSTRUCTIONS: Cover bowl and let dough ripen in cool place for at least 12 hours. Drop by teaspoon 3 inches apart, on greased cookie pans. Bake.

Oven Temperature: 350 degrees Fahrenheit.

Baking Time: 12 to 15 minutes.

Let cool on cake racks. When cool, frost with Decorating Icing II (Page 298). Top with toasted almond or pecan half, if desired. Store until ready to use. An apple in the cookie jar will keep cookies from drying out.

Makes about 10 dozen cookies.

12. LADYFINGERS

LADYFINGERS NO. 1

INGREDIENTS	METHOD
3 egg whites	*Beat until stiff but moist.*
⅓ cup fine granulated sugar	*Add gradually, continue beating.*
2 egg yolks	*Beat yolks until thick and lemon colored. Combine with sugar mixture.*
½ tsp. vanilla	*Add to above.*
⅓ cup all-purpose flour ⅛ tsp. salt	*Sift together, fold into egg mixture with large spoon.*
Confectioners' sugar	*Use as directed in instructions which follow.*

SPECIAL INSTRUCTIONS: Bake in ladyfinger tins, or use pastry bag and plain hole tube; shape 1- by 4-inch cookies on a cookie pan covered with brown paper. Sprinkle all over with confectioners' sugar. Bake.

Oven Temperature: 400 degrees Fahrenheit.

Baking Time: 8 to 10 minutes.

Remove from paper with spatula, or turn paper over (with ladyfingers on it) and wet the back of the paper lightly with a damp cloth. Then remove ladyfingers.

Makes 18 or more ladyfingers.

LADYFINGERS NO. 2

INGREDIENTS	METHOD
½ cup (4) egg whites	*Beat until whites stand in peaks.*
¼ tsp. cream of tartar	*Add and continue beating.*
5 tblsps. granulated sugar	*Add gradually, continue beating until very stiff.*
2 egg yolks ⅛ tsp. salt 1 tsp. vanilla	*In a separate bowl, beat until light. Add salt and flavoring.*
5 tblsps. granulated sugar	*Add to yolks and beat until thick. Add yolk mixture to whites mixture. Fold in.*
1¼ cups cake flour ½ tsp. baking powder	*Sift together. Carefully fold into the above and blend.*

SPECIAL INSTRUCTIONS: Form 4-inch-long fingers of dough on paper covered or well greased cookie pans. Or fill greased and well floured ladyfinger forms. Sift confectioners' sugar over all. Bake.

Oven Temperature: 400 degrees Fahrenheit.

Baking Time: 6 to 8 minutes.

Immediately remove ladyfingers with a spatula. Or turn paper upside-down and rub with a damp cloth until they come off easily.

Makes 36 or more ladyfingers.

PAN-CUT LADYFINGERS

INGREDIENTS	METHOD
6 egg yolks	*Beat.*
6 tblsps. milk ½ cup granulated sugar	*Add and beat until light and fluffy.*
3 cups all-purpose flour 2½ tsps. baking powder 1 tsp. salt	*Sift together and fold into egg mixture gradually.*
3 cups pitted dates, finely chopped 1½ cups finely chopped walnuts 1 tblsp. vanilla	*Add to above mixture.*
6 egg whites	*Beat stiff. Fold into above mixture.*

SPECIAL INSTRUCTIONS: Spread dough ½ inch thick on greased and floured cookie pans. Bake.

Oven Temperature: 350 degrees Fahrenheit.

Baking Time: approximately 30 minutes, or until it tests done. While still warm, cut with sharp knife into finger lengths. Sprinkle with confectioners' sugar. Let cool.

Makes 4 to 5 dozen ladyfingers.

13. LEMON COOKIES

LEMON DROP COOKIES

INGREDIENTS	METHOD
½ cup granulated sugar 1 tsp. grated lemon rind ½ cup margarine	*Cream well together.*
1 egg ⅓ cup honey	*Beat egg, blend with honey, add to above, mix well.*
2 cups all-purpose flour 1 tsp. baking powder 1 tsp. salt	*Sift together, add gradually to egg mixture. Blend to smooth dough.*

SPECIAL INSTRUCTIONS: Drop by teaspoon onto greased cookie pans. Flatten each cookie with floured fork. Decorate with chopped candied lemon peel. Bake.

Oven Temperature: 350 degrees Fahrenheit.

Baking Time: 10 to 12 minutes.

Makes about 3 dozen cookies.

LEMON BUTTER COOKIES

INGREDIENTS	METHOD
1 cup butter	*Cream.*
1½ cups granulated sugar	*Add gradually, cream together until light.*
2 eggs, well beaten 2 tblsps. lemon juice 1 tsp. lemon extract	*Add, blend well.*
4 cups all-purpose flour 3 tsps. baking powder ¾ tsp. salt	*Sift flour, baking powder and salt together, add to butter mixture and blend thoroughly.*
1 cup ground almonds 3 tsps. grated lemon rind	*Stir in and mix well.*

SPECIAL INSTRUCTIONS: Shape dough into a roll 2½ inches in diameter; wrap in waxed paper and chill in refrigerator at least 5 hours. To bake, cut roll in thin slices with a sharp serrated knife. Place on ungreased cookie pans at least 3 inches apart. Bake.

Oven Temperature: 400 degrees Fahrenheit.

Baking Time: 8 to 10 minutes.

Decorate with your favorite frosting or leave plain.

Makes about 48 cookies.

LEMON CRISPIES

INGREDIENTS	METHOD
1 cup margarine ½ cup granulated sugar ½ cup brown sugar	*Cream together.*
1 tblsp. lemon juice 1 egg	*Beat egg, add and beat well. Stir juice in.*
2½ cups all-purpose flour 1 tsp. salt ¼ tsp. baking soda	*Sift together and stir into above.*
1 tsp. grated lemon rind	*Stir into mixture.*

SPECIAL INSTRUCTIONS: Refrigerate dough until firm. Roll out to ⅛ inch thick. Cut with round cookie cutter. Brush each with mixture of 1 beaten egg, dash of salt and 2 tablespoons milk. Decorate with ½ candied cherry, or half pecan or walnut. Use spatula and place cookies on cookie pan. Bake.

Oven Temperature: 400 degrees Fahrenheit.

Baking Time: 10 to 12 minutes.

Makes about 2 dozen large cookies.

LEMON-CHEESE DIPS

INGREDIENTS	METHOD
1 cup butter 3-oz. package cream cheese	*Blend together.*
1 cup granulated sugar	*Add and mix well.*
1 egg 1 tblsp. lemon juice 1 tsp. finely chopped lemon rind	*Beat egg, add to above and mix. Add juice and rind. Stir together.*
1 tsp. baking powder 2½ cups all-purpose flour	*Sift together, add to egg mixture and blend thoroughly.*

SPECIAL INSTRUCTIONS: Press dough through pastry bag or cookie press into 2½-inch-long strips on lightly greased cookie pans. Bake.

Oven Temperature: 375 degrees Fahrenheit.

Baking Time: 8 to 10 minutes.

When baked, dip ends in Lemon Icing (Page 305) and then in finely chopped walnuts. Let cool.

Makes 30 or more cookies.

LEMON ROSETTES

INGREDIENTS	METHOD
½ cup butter ½ cup shortening	*Cream together until light.*
¾ cup granulated sugar	*Add gradually to butter mixture, beating well.*
2 eggs	*Beat, add and mix together 2 or 3 minutes.*
1 tsp. grated lemon rind 1 tsp. lemon extract ⅛ tsp. salt	*Add and blend into egg mixture.*
2¼ cups cake flour ½ tsp. baking powder	*Sift together, add gradually and mix to smooth dough.*

SPECIAL INSTRUCTIONS: With a cookie press or pastry bag with large star tube, make rosettes on lightly greased cookie pans. Bake.

Oven Temperature: 375 to 400 degrees Fahrenheit.

Baking Time: 10 to 12 minutes.

Makes about 3 dozen rosettes.

Lemon Sweets

LEMON SWEETS

INGREDIENTS	METHOD
½ cup butter 1 cup granulated sugar	*Cream together until light.*
2 eggs 1 tsp. vanilla	*Beat eggs, add and mix well.*
2 cups all-purpose flour ¼ tsp. baking soda ½ tsp. salt	*Sift together, add to egg mixture and blend.*
¼ cup lemon juice 1 tblsp. grated lemon rind	*Add to above and mix thoroughly.*
¼ cup Lemon Sugar (See page 305) Raspberry jam	*See instructions below.*

SPECIAL INSTRUCTIONS: Roll dough out on floured board or pastry cloth. Cut with 2-inch round cutter. Sprinkle each cookie with Lemon Sugar (Page 305). Dot some of them with raspberry jam. Bake.

Oven Temperature: 375 degrees Fahrenheit.

Baking Time: 15 minutes.

Makes about 2 dozen cookies.

14. MACAROONS

HOMEMADE ALMOND PASTE FOR MACAROONS

INGREDIENTS	METHOD
2 cups almonds (buy blanched almonds if possible, or see Method)	*Blanch almonds and dry thoroughly. Do not toast or dry in oven. Grind through finest blade of food chopper 3 times.*
1½ cups confectioners' sugar	*Sift sugar and mix with almonds.*
¼ cup (2 whites) egg whites 2 tsps. almond extract	*Add and mix thoroughly in blender.*

SPECIAL INSTRUCTIONS: Mold the paste into a ball. Place in tightly covered container and store in refrigerator at least 4 days to age.

Makes 1 pound, about 3½ cups.

ALMOND-PASTE MACAROONS

INGREDIENTS	METHOD
1 cup almond paste 1½ cups fine granulated sugar ½ cup (4 whites) un-beaten egg whites 1 tblsp. all-purpose flour	*Mix almond paste and sugar with a little egg white until smooth. Use blender for ease of handling. Add more egg white and mix smooth again. Add the rest of the egg white and the flour and mix well.*

SPECIAL INSTRUCTIONS: Drop from spoon onto cookie pans covered with thick paper. Bake.

Oven Temperature: 325 to 350 degrees Fahrenheit.

Baking Time: 18 to 20 minutes.

Let cool. Turn paper over and dampen it with a wet cloth until macaroons come off easily. Avoid soaking the paper.

Makes 16 or more large macaroons.

FRENCH MACAROONS

INGREDIENTS	METHOD
1 cup (purchased) almond paste ½ cup granulated sugar 1 egg white	*Mix to a smooth, medium stiff mixture. Use wooden spoon or blender.*
½ cup granulated sugar 1 to 2 egg whites	*Add and mix well for about 5 minutes by hand, or use blender 1 or 2 minutes.*

SPECIAL INSTRUCTIONS: Use pastry bag and No. 6 plain tube; squeeze out onto cookie pans covered with brown paper. Let stand 10 minutes. Bake.

Oven Temperature: 325 degrees Fahrenheit.

Baking Time: 25 to 30 minutes.

Let cool. Remove from paper by wetting back of paper with cloth wrung out of cold water. Finely chopped candied cherries may be added to mixture before baking. Tops may be decorated with almonds or bits of cherries.

Makes 24 or more large macaroons.

NEW ORLEANS MACAROONS

INGREDIENTS	METHOD
2 eggs	*Beat until light.*
1 cup granulated sugar	*Add gradually.*
5 tsps. melted butter 2 tsps. vanilla 2 tsps. almond extract 2½ cups uncooked oat- meal	*Add and mix thoroughly.*

SPECIAL INSTRUCTIONS: Spoon small amounts of mixture onto greased cookie pans 3 inches apart. Bake.

Oven Temperature: 325 degrees Fahrenheit.

Baking Time: 20 to 25 minutes.

Makes about 3 dozen macaroons.

COCONUT MACAROON GEMS

INGREDIENTS	METHOD
1 tblsp. cake flour ¼ tsp. salt ½ cup granulated sugar	*Combine flour, salt and sugar and sift into bowl.*
2 egg whites	*Beat until stiff and peaky, but not dry. Fold into flour mixture.*
½ tsp. vanilla	*Add.*
2 cups finely chopped or shredded coconut	*Fold in carefully.*

SPECIAL INSTRUCTIONS: Drop by teaspoon onto lightly greased waxed paper on cookie pans. Allow space for spreading. Bake.

Oven Temperature: 350 degrees Fahrenheit.

Baking Time: about 20 minutes, or until golden brown and dry on surface.

Makes about 32 cookies.

COCONUT MACAROON NESTS

INGREDIENTS	METHOD
3 egg whites ¾ cup granulated sugar ⅛ tsp. salt 1 tsp. vanilla 2 cups finely chopped or shredded coconut	*Combine all ingredients in a double boiler and mix until quite warm and pliable. Do not boil. Remove from heat.*

SPECIAL INSTRUCTIONS: Squeeze onto well greased cookie pans with pastry bag and large star tube; or drop by tablespoon onto the cookie pans. To make ridges around the dropped cookies, use a fork. Add a maraschino or candied cherry to the top of each. Bake.

Oven Temperature: 325 degrees Fahrenheit.

Baking Time: 15 to 20 minutes.

Makes about 30 nests.

FRENCH CRESCENT MACAROONS

INGREDIENTS	METHOD
1 cup almond paste ½ cup confectioners' sugar 1 egg white (variable)	*Cream together with wooden spoon. Or use blender.*
Finely chopped almonds	*Use as directed in instructions below.*

SPECIAL INSTRUCTIONS: Shape the soft mixture into a ½-inch-thick long roll. Cut pieces from roll each 3 inches long. Roll each piece in chopped almonds and shape into a crescent. (Also called a horn by European bakers.) Place on buttered cookie pans. Bake.

Oven Temperature: 300 degrees Fahrenheit.

Baking Time: 20 minutes.

Let cool and frost with Confectioners' Icing (Page 295). Make frosting thin enough to put on with a brush and flavor it with lemon juice until quite tart. Other nuts may be used in place of almonds.

Makes 12 or more crescents.

CHOCOLATE MACAROONS

INGREDIENTS	METHOD
1 cup (purchased) almond paste 1 egg white	*Mix together in blender.*
1¾ cups confectioners' sugar 1 egg white 1 cup confectioners' sugar ¼ cup cocoa powder	*Add sugar and egg white slowly to above and mix until smooth. Mix sugar and cocoa powder and add to above. Blend.*
1 egg white ¼ tsp. almond extract	*Add to above and blend in thoroughly.*

SPECIAL INSTRUCTIONS: Drop from teaspoon onto cookie pans covered with thick paper. Bake.

Oven Temperature: 350 degrees Fahrenheit.

Baking Time: 18 to 20 minutes.

Let cool. Remove macaroons from paper by dampening the back of the paper with a wet cloth.

Makes 70 or more macaroons.

EUROPEAN COCONUT MACAROONS

INGREDIENTS	METHOD
1 cup finely chopped unsweetened coconut 1½ cups fine granulated sugar ⅔ cup (6 or 7 whites) egg whites (variable) 1 tblsp. all-purpose flour	*Mix all ingredients together in top of double boiler and heat until quite warm. Do not boil. Remove from heat.*

SPECIAL INSTRUCTIONS: Use tablespoon and drop mixture immediately onto well greased and floured, or greased waxed paper covered, cookie pans. Bake.

Oven Temperature: 375 degrees Fahrenheit.

Baking Time: about 12 minutes.

For MINIATURE MACAROONS or MOUNDS, use same recipe but drop from teaspoon. Baking time 15 minutes in 350 degree Fahrenheit oven.

Makes 30 or more large macaroons.
Makes 60 or more small macaroons.

NUT MACAROONS

INGREDIENTS	METHOD
1 large egg white	*Beat until stiff.*
1 cup brown sugar	*Add gradually, continue to beat.*
1 cup finely chopped pecans Pinch of salt	*Cut and fold in.*

SPECIAL INSTRUCTIONS: Drop from teaspoon onto cookie pans covered with heavy paper. Bake.

Oven Temperature: 325 degrees Fahrenheit.

Baking Time: 20 to 25 minutes.

Let cool. Turn upside-down, wet paper with damp cloth and remove macaroons.

Makes about 1½ dozen.

15. MARZIPAN

MARZIPAN FRUIT PASTE

INGREDIENTS	METHOD
2 cups (1 lb.) almond paste 2 cups confectioners' sugar 2 or 3 egg whites 2 tblsps. white corn syrup 1 tsp. almond extract	*Mix all ingredients together until a smooth, stiff paste is obtained. Use blender at low speed.*

SPECIAL INSTRUCTIONS: Keep paste mixture in a covered jar to prevent crust from forming.

Makes about 4 cups paste.

MARZIPAN FRUIT AND VEGETABLES

For potatoes, radishes, white turnips, strawberries, use the plain white paste mixture.

For apples, use 1 or 2 drops red pure-food coloring.

For pears, peaches and bananas, use a little yellow pure-food coloring.

For carrots and pumpkins, use orange pure-food coloring.

METHOD: Roll small pieces of Marzipan Fruit Paste and shape into fruits or vegetables. Shape by hand and make the grooves and other identifying marks with a marzipan modeling set or a butter spreader. Natural looking leaves of the different fruits and vegetables are available from pastry and candy supply shops.

16. MERINGUES AND KISSES

NUT MERINGUES

INGREDIENTS	METHOD
2 egg whites	*Beat until very stiff and dry.*
¼ cup fine granulated sugar	*Add a spoonful at a time, whipping until it holds its shape.*
½ tsp. vanilla	*Add.*
¼ cup granulated sugar ½ cup chopped nuts	*Fold in gently.*

SPECIAL INSTRUCTIONS: Shape mixture into shells, bars, kisses, or any desired shapes on cookie pans covered with thick paper. Sprinkle with more chopped nuts. Bake.

Oven Temperature: 200 to 225 degrees Fahrenheit.

Baking Time: until meringues are very dry.

Remove from paper as described in Meringue Kisses I.

Makes about 12 to 16 meringues.

FANCY MERINGUE FIGURES I

INGREDIENTS	METHOD
½ cup (4 or 5 whites) egg whites Pinch of salt	*Beat until frothy.*
¼ tsp. cream of tartar	*Beat in.*
¾ cup granulated sugar	*Add by tablespoon, beating constantly.*
½ cup granulated sugar 1 tsp. vanilla	*Fold in gently.*

SPECIAL INSTRUCTIONS: Squeeze meringue with pastry bag and No. 3 star tube into fancy designs onto a cookie pan covered with thick paper. Sprinkle the figures with Colored Sugar (Page 305). Bake.

Oven Temperature: 225 degrees Fahrenheit.

Baking Time: 30 to 40 minutes, or until they are dry and crisp. Let cool slightly. Remove from the paper to a cake rack to dry.

NOTE: If meringue figures are to be hung on a Christmas tree, insert a small loop of string or fine wire in them before baking.

Makes 10 or more meringues.

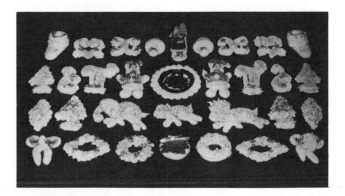

MERINGUE FIGURES II

INGREDIENTS	METHOD
½ cup (4 or 5 whites) egg whites	*Beat until dry.*
1½ cups granulated sugar	*Add gradually and beat until mixture holds its shape.*
¾ tsp. vanilla ¾ tsp. vinegar	*Add and beat until well incorporated.*

SPECIAL INSTRUCTIONS: Use plain, medium size decorating tube and canvas or paper pastry bag. Shape meringue into such figures as booties, hearts, trees, bells, animals, harps, bows, wreaths, etc., on cookie pans covered with thick paper. Sprinkle with Colored Sugar (Page 305), or decorate as you choose. Bake in a slow oven.

Oven Temperature: 225 degrees Fahrenheit.

Baking Time: until thoroughly dried out.

Let cool. Remove from paper. Keep baked figures dry at all times. Tie a string to each and hang on the Christmas tree. This meringue can also be made into kisses. Drop from a spoon onto a cookie pan covered with thick paper. Add candied fruit, nuts and raisins to the meringue before baking. This meringue mixture also can be used to make meringue shells.

Makes 12 to 18 kisses; 30 or more small figures; 10 to 12 meringue shells.

MERINGUE KISSES I

INGREDIENTS	METHOD
2 egg whites	*Beat until very stiff and dry.*
¼ cup fine granulated sugar	*Add spoonful at a time. Continue beating until mixture holds its shape.*
1 tsp. vanilla	*Add.*
¼ cup fine granulated sugar ⅓ cup finely crushed nut brittle *	*Fold in.*

SPECIAL INSTRUCTIONS: Form into desired shapes on cookie pans covered with thick paper. Sprinkle with shredded almonds and sift confectioners' sugar over them. Bake. (Also see preceding recipe.)

Oven Temperature: 250 degrees Fahrenheit.

Baking Time: 30 to 35 minutes, or until set and delicately browned.

Remove paper with baked kisses on it. Lay wet towel on hot cookie pan and place paper with kisses on towel. Let stand 1 minute and steam will loosen kisses. Slip them off the paper with a spatula. Let dry.

Makes 24 or more kisses.

* Nut brittle made with almonds is preferred.

MERINGUE KISSES II

INGREDIENTS	METHOD
2 egg whites	*Beat in mixing bowl, until frothy.*
¼ tsp. salt	*Add, continue beating until whites are whipped dry.*
1 cup granulated sugar	*Add gradually, beat until mixture holds stiff peaks.*
1½ cups shredded coconut ½ tsp. vanilla	*Fold in gently.*

SPECIAL INSTRUCTIONS: Drop by teaspoon 1½ inches apart on lightly greased cookie pans. Bake.

Oven Temperature: 275 degrees Fahrenheit.

Baking Time: 15 to 20 minutes, or until set and delicately browned.

For PINK MERINGUE KISSES, add 1 or 2 drops pink pure-food coloring to meringue mixture before baking.

Makes 18 to 24 kisses.

Meringue Nests and Shells

MERINGUE NESTS AND SHELLS

INGREDIENTS	METHOD
2 egg whites	*Beat until very stiff and dry.*
½ cup granulated sugar	*Beat in ¼ cup of sugar, spoonful at a time.*
Pinch of salt	*Add, beat until mixture holds its shape.*
½ tsp. vanilla	*Add and then fold in remaining ¼ cup sugar.*

SPECIAL INSTRUCTIONS: Shape with spoon or with pastry bag and tube into nests on a cookie pan covered with heavy paper. Bake.

Oven Temperature: 225 degrees Fahrenheit.

Baking Time: 50 to 60 minutes.

Remove from paper. If the nests stick to the paper, wipe back of paper with a damp cloth.

Makes 12 nests.

MERINGUE GLACÉES: Arrange flat ovals of meringue or shape in 3-inch oval rings or shells on a wet board covered with thick paper toweling. Bake as above until crisp and dry. Remove from paper and let cool. When cold, crush center or remove soft center with teaspoon. Put together in pairs with whipped cream or ice cream. Serve with crushed strawberries, a chocolate sauce, Strawberry Whip (Page 307), or other sauces.

Makes 12 or more.

DATE AND NUT MERINGUES

INGREDIENTS	METHOD
2 egg whites	*Beat until very stiff and dry.*
¼ cup fine granulated sugar	*Add, spoonful at a time, beat until mixture holds its shape.*
½ tsp. vanilla	*Add.*
¼ cup fine granulated sugar ½ cup chopped pecans ¼ lb. pitted and finely cut dates (⅔ cup)	*Fold in.*

SPECIAL INSTRUCTIONS: Use pastry bag and large plain or star tube. Form mixture into any designs or shapes desired on cookie pans greased and covered with waxed paper. Bake.

Oven Temperature: 300 degrees Fahrenheit.

Baking Time: 35 minutes.

This meringue is especially good when made into shells and filled with ice cream.

Makes 12 shells, or 18 or more small meringues.

17. OATMEAL COOKIES

BOILED COOKIES

INGREDIENTS	METHOD
⅔ cup crunchy peanut butter 3 cups quick-cooking oatmeal	*Have ready to use, but set aside. Pour uncooked oatmeal into large bowl.*
2 cups granulated sugar 6 tblsps. cocoa powder ½ cup margarine 1 tsp. vanilla ½ cup milk	*Combine in saucepan and boil together for 3 minutes.*

SPECIAL INSTRUCTIONS: Remove sugar-cocoa mixture from heat and stir peanut butter into it. Pour into the oatmeal bowl and mix well. Drop by ½ teaspoon onto pans covered with waxed paper or foil. Bake.

Oven Temperature: 350 degrees Fahrenheit.

Baking Time: 10 minutes, or until done.

Let cool.

Makes about 15 dozen drop cookies.

CRUNCHY OATMEAL COOKIES

INGREDIENTS	METHOD
⅓ cup shortening ⅓ cup brown sugar ⅓ cup granulated sugar	*Cream all together until light.*
1 egg 1 tsp. vanilla	*Beat egg, add with vanilla and mix together until smooth.*
¼ tsp. salt ½ tsp. baking powder 1 cup uncooked oatmeal 2 tblsps. all-purpose flour ½ cup finely chopped nuts	*Sift flour, baking powder and salt together. Add with oatmeal to egg mixture. Combine well. Add nuts and mix in.*

SPECIAL INSTRUCTIONS: Drop by level tablespoon, 3 inches apart, onto ungreased cookie pans. Bake.

Oven Temperature: 350 degrees Fahrenheit.

Baking Time: 8 to 10 minutes, or until cookies are light brown. Let cookies cool 2 or 3 minutes before removing from pan. Cookies will be thin and lacy.

Makes 40 cookies.

COCONUT OATMEAL COOKIES

INGREDIENTS	METHOD
½ cup all-purpose flour ½ tsp. salt ⅔ cup granulated sugar	*Sift together into mixing bowl.*
1 cup soft shortening 2 eggs ½ tsp. vanilla 1 tsp. grated orange rind	*Cut shortening in with pastry blender or 2 knives. Beat eggs, add with vanilla and orange rind.*
1 cup uncooked oatmeal ½ cup moist grated or shredded coconut	*Fold into egg mixture and blend completely.*

SPECIAL INSTRUCTIONS: Drop by teaspoon 2 inches apart onto cookie pans. Flatten slightly with spatula which has been dipped in cold water. Bake.

Oven Temperature: 350 to 375 degrees Fahrenheit.

Baking Time: 10 to 12 minutes.

Remove cookies from pans immediately. Let cool.

Makes about 96 drop cookies.

LIGHT-BROWN OATMEAL COOKIES

INGREDIENTS	METHOD
1 cup butter or margarine	*Melt, remove from heat.*
1½ cups light brown sugar	*Beat with butter or margarine.*
2¼ cups uncooked oatmeal	*Add butter-and-sugar mixture to oatmeal. Let stand overnight at room temperature.*
½ tsp. salt 3 tblsps. all-purpose flour 1 tblsp. molasses, if desired 1 slightly beaten egg 1 tsp. vanilla	*Sift flour and salt together. Add alternately with molasses, egg and vanilla. Mix well with oatmeal.*
Milk Pecan halves	*Use as described in instructions below.*

SPECIAL INSTRUCTIONS: Drop level teaspoons of dough 2 inches apart on heavily greased and floured cookie pans. Brush tops lightly with milk. Press a pecan half on the center of each cookie. Bake.

Oven Temperature: 375 degrees Fahrenheit.

Baking Time: 5 to 7 minutes, or until brown around the edges. After removing from oven, let cookies remain on pan a few minutes until firm. Then immediately remove with spatula to cooling rack.

Makes 100 or more drop cookies.

NUT OATMEAL COOKIES

INGREDIENTS	METHOD
¾ cup butter ¼ cup shortening 1 cup confectioners' sugar	*Cream together until light.*
1 tsp. vanilla 1 tsp. almond extract ¼ tsp. salt	*Add and mix.*
1¼ cups all-purpose flour 1 cup uncooked oatmeal	*Sift flour, add with oatmeal to butter mixture. Combine smoothly.*
Finely chopped nuts	*Use as described in instructions below.*

SPECIAL INSTRUCTIONS: Divide dough in half. Shape into 2 rolls. Dip each in finely chopped nuts and wrap in waxed paper. Chill for several hours or overnight. Slice in thin slices and bake on lightly greased cookie pans.

Oven Temperature: 375 degrees Fahrenheit.

Baking Time: 10 to 12 minutes.

Makes 96 or more cookies.

OATMEAL ROUNDS

INGREDIENTS	METHOD
2 cups brown sugar ½ cup margarine ½ cup shortening 1 tsp. salt	*Cream all together until light.*
1 egg 1 tsp. vanilla	*Beat egg, add with vanilla and blend in well.*
¼ cup all-purpose flour 2¼ cups quick-cooking oatmeal	*Add uncooked oatmeal and sifted flour to egg mixture and blend into a medium stiff dough.*

SPECIAL INSTRUCTIONS: If dough is too soft to roll, place in the refrigerator for 30 to 40 minutes. Then roll dough out into ⅛-inch thickness. Cut with a 2½ or 3-inch round cookie cutter. Place 2 inches apart on lightly greased cookie pans, brush with a mixture of 1 egg, 2 tablespoons milk, and a pinch of salt. Bake.

Oven Temperature: 375 degrees Fahrenheit.

Baking Time: 8 to 10 minutes, or until done.

Makes about 50 cookies.

RAISIN OATMEAL COOKIES

INGREDIENTS	METHOD
1 cup granulated sugar ½ cup shortening	*Cream together.*
2 eggs	*Beat in 1 at a time.*
¼ cup milk 2 cups quick-cooking oatmeal 1 cup washed and drained seedless raisins	*Add uncooked oatmeal, alternating with milk. Mix raisins in.*
1½ cups all-purpose flour 1 tsp. baking soda ½ tsp. salt 1 tsp. powdered cinnamon	*Sift together, add and blend.*

SPECIAL INSTRUCTIONS: Let dough remain in refrigerator about 1 hour. Roll out ⅛ inch thick on floured board. Cut with 2 or 3-inch round cookie cutter, plain or scalloped. Brush with milk, or mixture of 1 egg, 2 tablespoons milk and pinch of salt. Bake.

Oven Temperature: 350 degrees Fahrenheit.

Baking Time: 12 to 15 minutes.

NOTE: This dough can also be baked as drop cookies. In which case, it is unnecessary to chill the dough. The drop cookies will take a little longer to bake than the cut-out cookies.

Makes about 60 rolled cookies; 80 or more drop cookies.

POWDER-PUFF TIDBITS

INGREDIENTS	METHOD
1 cup shortening 1 cup brown sugar 1 cup granulated sugar	*Cream together.*
2 eggs 1 tsp. vanilla	*Beat eggs, add and mix well.*
2 cups all-purpose flour 1 tsp. baking soda ½ tsp. baking powder ½ tsp. salt	*Sift together.*
2 cups quick-cooking oatmeal	*Add uncooked oatmeal together with flour to egg mixture and blend well.*
6 oz. chocolate chips 1 cup finely shredded or chopped coconut 14 to 16 finely chopped maraschino cherries	*Melt chocolate, add with coconut and cherries to dough.*

SPECIAL INSTRUCTIONS: Drop from teaspoon onto greased cookie pans. Bake.

Oven Temperature: 375 degrees Fahrenheit.

Baking Time: 10 to 12 minutes.

When cool leave single or put 2 cookies together with jam and sift confectioners' sugar over.

Makes 15 or 16 dozen tidbits.

CHOCOLATE OATMEAL COOKIES

INGREDIENTS	METHOD
1½ cups butter or margarine 2 tsps. vanilla	*Cream together.*
2 cups brown sugar	*Add sugar to butter or margarine and cream well.*
4 eggs	*Add 1 at a time, beating well after each addition.*
2 cups all-purpose flour 2 tsps. baking powder 1 tsp. salt	*Sift together.*
⅔ cup milk	*Blend into the egg mixture alternately with the sifted flour.*
6 cups uncooked oatmeal	*Stir into the above mixture.*
2 cups chocolate bits 2 cups chopped walnuts or pecans	*Melt chocolate over hot water. Add with nuts to oatmeal dough.*

SPECIAL INSTRUCTIONS: Drop from teaspoon onto greased cookie pans. Bake.

Oven Temperature: 375 degrees Fahrenheit.

Baking Time: 12 to 15 minutes.

Makes more than 20 dozen drop cookies.

DATE OATMEAL COOKIES

INGREDIENTS	METHOD
1 cup shortening 1½ cups dark brown sugar	*Cream together until light and fluffy.*
2 eggs	*Beat and add. Mix to blend well.*
2 cups all-purpose flour ½ tsp. salt ½ tsp. baking soda 2 tsps. baking powder	*Sift together.*
1½ cups uncooked oatmeal	*Mix with flour.*
⅔ cup buttermilk	*Add to egg mixture alternately with flour mixture.*
1 cup pitted dates, finely chopped 1 cup chopped pecans 1 tsp. peanut butter 1 tsp. vanilla	*Fold in and blend.*

SPECIAL INSTRUCTIONS: Drop from teaspoon onto greased and floured cookie pans. Bake.

Oven Temperature: 350 degrees Fahrenheit.

Baking Time: about 10 to 12 minutes, or until delicately browned.

Makes about 18 dozen drops.

OATMEAL GEMS

INGREDIENTS	METHOD
¾ cup margarine or shortening ½ cup granulated sugar 1 cup brown sugar	*Cream together well.*
2 eggs	*Beat eggs, add and blend thoroughly.*
½ tsp. lemon extract	*Add and blend.*
1½ cups all-purpose flour ½ tsp. salt ½ tsp. baking soda ½ tsp. powdered cinnamon	*Sift together.*
1 cup quick-cooking oatmeal	*Add uncooked oatmeal gradually with flour to egg mixture.*
1 cup seedless raisins	*Wash and drain. Add and mix into dough.*

SPECIAL INSTRUCTIONS: Drop from teaspoon on ungreased cookie pans. Bake.

Oven Temperature: 375 degrees Fahrenheit.

Baking Time: 12 to 15 minutes.

Makes about 10 dozen gems.

BLACK-EYED SUSANS

INGREDIENTS	METHOD
½ cup shortening ¾ cup light brown sugar	*Cream together.*
1 egg 1 tsp. vanilla	*Beat egg, add with flavoring and mix well.*
¾ cup all-purpose flour ½ tsp. salt	*Sift together.*
1¼ cups quick-cooking oatmeal ¾ cup finely shredded or chopped coconut	*Add uncooked oatmeal with flour mixture and coconut. Blend thoroughly.*
Prune or apricot preserves	*Use as described in instructions below.*

SPECIAL INSTRUCTIONS: Chill dough thoroughly. Shape into small balls and roll in shredded or chopped coconut. Place on greased cookie pans and make a dent in top of each cookie with the handle of a knife. Fill dent with prune or apricot preserves. Bake.

Oven Temperature: 300 degrees Fahrenheit.

Baking Time: 25 to 30 minutes.

Let cool. Prune and apricot fillings are available in many large food stores.

Makes 40 or more cookies.

BROWN-SUGAR ORANGE OATMEAL COOKIES

INGREDIENTS	METHOD
1 cup shortening 2 cups brown sugar	*Cream together until light and fluffy.*
2 eggs	*Beat, add and continue mixing until well blended.*
½ tsp. salt 1 tsp. baking soda 2 cups all-purpose flour	*Sift together and add to egg mixture.*
⅓ cup orange juice 3 tsps. grated orange rind 2 cups uncooked oatmeal 1 cup pitted and chopped dates ½ cup chopped walnuts	*Add orange juice and oatmeal alternately to flour mixture, combining well. Add rind, dates and walnuts.*

SPECIAL INSTRUCTIONS: Drop by teaspoon on greased and floured cookie pans. Bake.

Oven Temperature: 375 degrees Fahrenheit.

Baking Time: 15 to 20 minutes.

Let cool.

Makes about 15 dozen drop cookies.

OATMEAL DROPS

INGREDIENTS	METHOD
½ cup margarine 1 cup light, sifted brown sugar	*Cream together until light.*
1 egg 1 tsp. rum flavoring	*Beat egg, add with flavoring and continue to beat for 2 minutes.*
¾ cup all-purpose flour ½ tsp. salt ½ tsp. baking soda	*Sift together and add.*
1½ cups quick-cooking oatmeal	*Mix uncooked oatmeal into dough until all ingredients are well blended.*

SPECIAL INSTRUCTIONS: Drop by teaspoon onto lightly greased and floured cookie pans. Bake.

Oven Temperature: 350 degrees Fahrenheit.

Baking Time: about 15 minutes.

Makes 60 to 70 drops.

18. PEANUT COOKIES

CRUNCHY PEANUT COOKIES

INGREDIENTS	METHOD
¾ cup shortening or margarine 1½ cups light brown sugar	*Cream fat and sugar together.*
1 egg, well beaten	*Beat into sugar mixture.*
½ tsp. salt ½ tsp. baking soda 2½ cups all-purpose flour	*Sift together.*
¾ cup ground peanuts 3 tblsps. milk	*Beat in with the sifted ingredients to sugar mixture.*

SPECIAL INSTRUCTIONS: Drop in portions the size of walnuts onto cookie pans. Bake.

Oven Temperature: 400 degrees Fahrenheit.

Baking Time: 12 to 15 minutes.

Makes 3½ to 4 dozen cookies.

PEANUT CUTOUTS

INGREDIENTS	METHOD
1 cup margarine	*Cream.*
2 cups fine granulated sugar	*Add to margarine and cream lightly.*
2 eggs	*Beat in 1 at a time.*
¼ cup milk 3½ cups all-purpose flour ¼ tsp. baking soda 1 tsp. baking powder ½ tsp. salt 1 cup finely ground peanuts 2 tsps. grated orange rind	*Sift flour, soda and salt together. Add alternately with milk only until flour has disappeared and dough is smooth. Fold nuts and orange rind in.*
Chocolate shots	*Use as directed in instructions below.*

SPECIAL INSTRUCTIONS: Roll dough about ¼ inch thick on flour dusted cloth. Cut with a round cookie cutter. Brush top with mixture of 2 tablespoons milk, dash of salt and 1 beaten egg. Sprinkle cookies with chocolate shots. Place on cookie pans. Bake.

Oven Temperature: 385 degrees Fahrenheit.

Baking Time: 12 to 15 minutes.

Other toppings such as nuts, colored sugar and shredded coconut can be used in place of chocolate shots. Or use Colored Sugar (Page 305).

Makes 72 to 80 cookies.

PEANUT-BUTTER ROSETTES

INGREDIENTS	METHOD
½ cup butter ½ cup granulated sugar ½ cup firmly packed brown sugar	*Cream together until fluffy.*
1 egg ½ cup peanut butter * ½ tsp. vanilla ¼ cup milk	*Beat in egg, peanut butter and vanilla. Add milk alternately with sifted flour.*
1¼ cups all-purpose flour ½ tsp. baking soda	*Sift together, add to above and mix until blended.*

SPECIAL INSTRUCTIONS: Force dough through cookie press, using any plate. Or use a pastry decorating tube and bag to make desired shapes on greased cookie pans. Decorate top of cookies with a blanched almond. Or brush the top with water and sprinkle with finely chopped peanuts before baking.

Oven Temperature: 350 degrees Fahrenheit.

Baking Time: about 12 minutes.

Makes 3 or 4 dozen cookies.

* Use smooth style peanut butter in this recipe.

*Peanut
Cutouts*

*Peanut-
Butter
Rosettes*

PEANUT CUTUPS

INGREDIENTS	METHOD
½ cup butter or shortening	*Cream.*
½ cup brown sugar	*Add gradually, cream together.*
1 egg, beaten 1 tsp. vanilla	*Add and mix well.*
½ cup finely chopped salted peanuts	*Add to above.*
1 cup all-purpose flour ½ tsp. powdered cinnamon ¼ tsp. baking soda	*Sift and add to above. Mix well.*
Coarsely chopped peanuts	*Use as directed in instructions below.*

SPECIAL INSTRUCTIONS: Spread or pat dough on greased cookie pan to a 14- by 10-inch rectangle. Brush with mixture of 1 egg beaten with 2 tablespoons milk and a dash of salt. Sprinkle dough with coarsely chopped peanuts. Bake.

Oven Temperature: 325 degrees Fahrenheit.

Baking Time: 20 to 25 minutes.

Cut in serving sized pieces while still warm.

Makes 35 2-inch squares.

19. PECAN COOKIES

PECAN KRISPIES

INGREDIENTS	METHOD
1 cup butter 1 cup granulated sugar ¼ tsp. powdered cinnamon ½ tsp. vanilla	*Cream all together.*
2 eggs	*Beat in 1 at a time. Mix well.*
2 cups all-purpose flour	*Sift, add and blend.*
½ cup Rice Krispies (cereal) ½ cup chopped pecans	*Add and combine with dough.*

SPECIAL INSTRUCTIONS: Make a long roll of this dough. Cut in small slices. Or drop dough by teaspoon onto lightly greased and floured cookie pans. Make a small dent in the center of each cookie and fill with a dot of raspberry jam. Bake.

Oven Temperature: 375 degrees Fahrenheit.

Baking Time: 12 to 15 minutes.

Makes about 50 slices (flat cookies) or 60 or more drop cookies.

PECAN PEANUT-BUTTER COOKIES

INGREDIENTS	METHOD
½ cup butter	*Cream.*
½ cup brown sugar	*Add gradually, cream together until light and fluffy.*
½ cup dark corn syrup ½ cup peanut butter ½ cup chopped pecans	*Add, beat until well blended.*
1 egg, well beaten ½ tsp. vanilla	*Add and blend.*
1⅔ cups all-purpose flour 1½ tsps. baking powder ⅛ tsp. salt	*Sift together, add a little at a time, mix well after each addition.*

SPECIAL INSTRUCTIONS: Shape dough into balls, about 1 inch in diameter. Place on lightly greased cookie pans, flatten cookies a little with a floured fork. Bake.

Oven Temperature: 350 degrees Fahrenheit.

Baking Time: 12 to 15 minutes.

Makes about 40 cookies.

PECAN SQUARES

INGREDIENTS	METHOD
2 eggs	*Beat.*
2 cups light brown sugar	*Beat into eggs gradually until well mixed.*
¼ tsp. salt ½ tsp. baking soda ⅔ cup all-purpose flour 1 cup chopped pecans	*Sift flour, baking soda and salt together. Add gradually, beating well to egg mixture. Add pecans.*

SPECIAL INSTRUCTIONS: Pour into greased shallow 9-inch square pan. Bake.
Oven Temperature: 375 degrees Fahrenheit.
Baking Time: 20 to 25 minutes.
When cool, cut into squares.
Makes 16 large squares.

*Pecan
Peanut-Butter
Cookies*

PECAN DELIGHTS

INGREDIENTS	METHOD
½ cup margarine	*Cream until fluffy.*
1 cup brown sugar	*Add gradually, cream until smooth.*
1 egg ¼ tsp. vanilla	*Beat in.*
2 cups all-purpose flour ½ tsp. baking soda ½ tsp. cream of tartar ¼ tsp. salt	*Sift together, add to egg mixture in fourths. Mix well after each addition.*
½ cup chopped pecans	*Fold in.*
Nuts for decoration	*See instructions below.*

SPECIAL INSTRUCTIONS: Divide dough in half. Shape into 2 rolls. Wrap each in waxed paper. Chill until very firm. Slice thin onto ungreased cookie pans. Bake.

Oven Temperature: 375 degrees Fahrenheit.

Baking Time: 8 to 10 minutes.

Let cool. Frost with Topping (opposite) and press pecan half into center of each cookie.

Makes 50 or more cookies.

PECAN DELIGHTS TOPPING	
INGREDIENTS	METHOD
3 tblsps. margarine	*Let stand at room temperature until soft. Do not melt.*
1 cup confectioners' sugar	*Sift, add gradually, beat with spoon.*
1½ tblsps. milk	*Add as needed to make frosting hold its shape when dropped from a spoon.*
½ tsp. vanilla	*Stir in.*

SPECIAL INSTRUCTIONS: From tip of teaspoon, drop about ½ teaspoon of topping in center of each cookie. Press a pecan half into the icing.

Makes about 1¼ cups topping.

20. PETITS FOURS

PETITS FOURS (cake part)

INGREDIENTS	METHOD
10 tblsps. shortening (½ cup plus 2 tblsps.) 2½ cups all-purpose flour	*Work together with pastry blender or 2 knives until fine crumbs.*
1½ cups granulated sugar ½ tsp. salt 2½ tsps. baking powder ¾ cup milk	*Sift sugar, salt and baking powder together. Add to flour mixture gradually with the milk.*
¾ cup (6 whites) egg whites	*Beat until stiff.*
½ cup milk 1 tsp. lemon extract	*Combine, mix half into flour mixture and blend. Then add the remaining half and mix for 6 minutes. Fold beaten egg whites into the batter.*

SPECIAL INSTRUCTIONS: Pour batter into a pan, 11½ by 17½ inches, greased, lined with waxed paper and buttered. Bake.

Oven Temperature: 375 degrees Fahrenheit.

Baking Time: 25 to 30 minutes.

For "Make-up" see page 231.

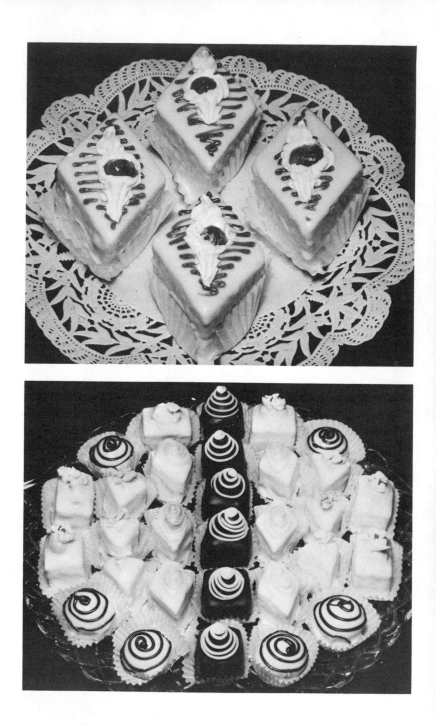

PETITS FOURS (make-up)

After the cake has been baked and cooled, it can be cut in half, ½ spread with jam, jelly, pastry cream or butter cream of any favorite flavor. Place top layer on the filling. Then cut this 2-layer cake into small shapes, such as stars, circles, oblongs, squares, diamonds, hearts, rounds, etc. Make certain that no crust remains on the cut shapes. Place them on a wire cake rack or screen, which has been set in a cookie pan to catch the excess icing. Pour Fondant Icing (Page 290) over them, being sure to cover each completely. The fondant icing must be dry before starting the decorating. Decorate in any manner you choose, using Decorating Icing (Page 297). For fancier Petits Fours, squeeze a mound of butter cream onto the top of each one after it has been filled and cut. Chill in the refrigerator until the butter cream becomes quite hard and solid. Then proceed as with the plainer cakes. These delicious cakes can be iced and decorated to suit the occasion or holiday: green icing and red decorations for Christmas, white icing and pastel blue or pink for baby showers, red icing and white decorations for St. Valentine's Day, and so forth.

21. POPPY-SEED COOKIES

POPPY-SEED WAFERS

INGREDIENTS	METHOD
1 cup cake flour	*Sift into a bowl.*
1 cup whole-wheat flour ½ tsp. salt 1 tblsp. granulated sugar	*Stir whole-wheat flour, salt and sugar into the cake flour.*
¼ cup shortening	*Cut shortening in with pastry blender or knives.*
Ice water	*Add enough to flour mixture to hold together when pressed lightly.*
Poppy seed	*Use as directed in instructions below.*

SPECIAL INSTRUCTIONS: Roll dough out ⅛ inch thick on a floured board. Brush lightly with milk, or with a mixture of 2 tablespoons milk, dash of salt, and 1 beaten egg. Sprinkle dough with poppy seed. Cut with a knife or pastry wheel into 1-inch squares. Or use a round or crescent cookie cutter and cut out cookies. Transfer with a spatula to greased cookie pans. Bake.

Oven Temperature: 375 degrees Fahrenheit.

Baking Time: 4 to 5 minutes, or until brown.

Let cool. Store in a covered container.

VARIATIONS: Caraway seed, celery or sesame seed may be substituted for the poppy seed.

Makes about 140 small square cookies or 60 or more rounds or crescents.

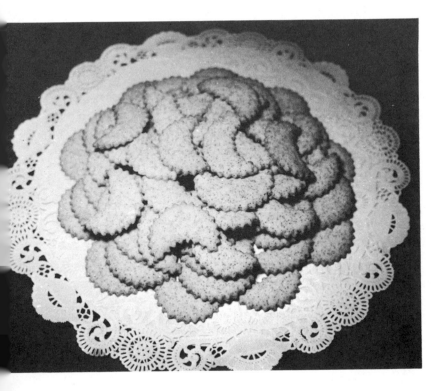

PUMPKIN POPPY-SEED COOKIES

INGREDIENTS	METHOD
¾ cup butter 1⅓ cups granulated sugar	*Cream together thoroughly.*
1 egg	*Beat into sugar mixture.*
1 cup cooked and mashed pumpkin ¼ cup light molasses 1 tsp. vanilla	*Combine and stir into egg-sugar mixture.*
2½ cups all-purpose flour 1 tsp. baking powder 1 tsp. baking soda 1 tsp. salt	*Sift together. Add to above and blend until smooth.*
1 cup finely chopped pecans ⅓ cup poppy seed	*Blend in.*

SPECIAL INSTRUCTIONS: Drop by rounded teaspoon onto greased cookie pans. Bake.

Oven Temperature: 350 degrees Fahrenheit.

Baking Time: 10 to 12 minutes.

Let cool. Frost with Pecan Frosting (Page 301). Top each with pecan half or leave plain.

Makes about 100 drop cookies.

CHOCOLATE POPPY-SEED COOKIES

INGREDIENTS	METHOD
1 cup poppy seeds ½ cup scalded milk	*Soak seeds in the milk for ½ hour.*
½ cup butter or margarine 1 cup granulated sugar	*Cream well together.*
1 egg yolk	*Beat yolk into sugar mixture.*
2 oz. (squares) unsweetened chocolate 1½ cups all-purpose flour 1 tsp. baking powder ⅛ tsp. salt ½ tsp. powdered cinnamon ¼ tsp. ground cloves ¼ cup currants (optional) ¼ cup washed, drained, chopped seedless raisins (optional)	*Melt chocolate over hot water. Sift flour with baking powder, salt, cinnamon and cloves. Add, beating, to egg-sugar mixture. Add currants and raisins. When all is well blended, add the soaked poppy seeds. Mix evenly.*

SPECIAL INSTRUCTIONS: Drop by teaspoon onto greased cookie pans. Bake.

Oven Temperature: 350 degrees Fahrenheit.

Baking Time: 20 minutes.

Makes about 10 dozen drop cookies.

TASTY POPPY-SEED COOKIES

INGREDIENTS	METHOD
1 cup butter	*Beat until very creamy.*
2 cups all-purpose flour	*Sift and mix into above, combining well.*
6 tblsps. granulated sugar 5 tblsps. rice flour 2 tsps. poppy seed	*Mix together and blend into above thoroughly.*

SPECIAL INSTRUCTIONS: Roll on floured board to ½-inch thickness. Cut into desired shapes. Place on lightly greased and floured cookie pans. Bake.

Oven Temperature: 275 degrees Fahrenheit.

Baking Time: 30 to 35 minutes, or until faintly brown.

Makes about 36 cookies.

22. REFRIGERATOR COOKIES

REFRIGERATOR DAINTIES

INGREDIENTS	METHOD
½ cup butter 1 cup brown sugar 2 egg yolks ⅛ tsp. salt ½ tsp. vanilla	*Cream butter and sugar together. Beat yolks, add with salt and flavoring.*
½ tsp. baking soda ½ tsp. cream of tartar 2 cups all-purpose flour	*Sift dry ingredients. Add gradually, mixing well.*
½ cup chopped walnuts ¼ cup washed and drained seedless raisins	*Add and mix into a medium stiff dough.*

SPECIAL INSTRUCTIONS: Shape dough into 2 long rolls, or pour into a 9-inch square pan lined with waxed paper. Refrigerate until stiff. Slice in ⅛-inch slices. Place on greased cookie pans. Bake.

Oven Temperature: 350 degrees Fahrenheit.

Baking Time: 8 to 10 minutes.

Makes about 64 cookies.

FANTASY REFRIGERATOR COOKIES

INGREDIENTS	METHOD
2 cups butter or margarine 2 cups sifted confectioners' sugar 2 tsps. vanilla	*Cream together thoroughly.*
4½ cups all-purpose flour ½ tsp. salt	*Sift together, stir in until well blended.*
1 oz. (square) unsweetened chocolate Pure-food coloring	*Melt chocolate (if using) and add to ½ of mixture. Or add a few drops coloring.*

SPECIAL INSTRUCTIONS: Mix the 2 portions (plain and chocolate) together, but do not blend. The colors should remain distinct. Shape into roll about 2 inches in diameter. The dough will have a marbled effect. Wrap in waxed paper; chill several hours or overnight. Cut slices about ⅛ inch thick. Place on ungreased cookie pans, a little apart from each other. Bake.

Oven Temperature: 400 degrees Fahrenheit.

Baking Time: 8 to 10 minutes, or until very delicate brown.

Makes about 6½ dozen cookies.

REFRIGERATOR SHADOW COOKIES

INGREDIENTS	METHOD
1 cup margarine 2 cups granulated sugar	*Cream together thoroughly.*
2 eggs 1 tsp. almond extract 1 tsp. vanilla	*Beat eggs, add and blend well.*
3½ cups all-purpose flour ½ tsp. salt 2 tsps. baking powder	*Sift together, add and blend well.*
1 oz. (square) un- sweetened chocolate	*Melt over hot water. Use as described in instructions below.*

SPECIAL INSTRUCTIONS: Form ½ of mixture into long roll about 2 inches in diameter. Wrap in waxed paper and chill in refrigerator until firm. Add the melted chocolate to the remaining ½ of dough, form into long roll and place in refrigerator until firm. Slice both rolls into ⅛-inch-thick cookies. Place on cookie pans and bake.

Oven Temperature: 375 degrees Fahrenheit.

Baking Time: 10 to 12 minutes.

Makes about 68 cookies.

PLAIN REFRIGERATOR COOKIES

INGREDIENTS	METHOD
½ cup shortening 1 cup granulated sugar * 1 egg 2 tsps. vanilla **	*Mix together until creamy.*
1½ cups all-purpose flour ½ tsp. baking soda ¾ tsp. salt	*Sift together, add to egg mixture and blend.*
½ cup chopped nuts (optional)	*Add to mixture.*

SPECIAL INSTRUCTIONS: Turn dough onto large piece of waxed paper. Shape into roll about 2 inches in diameter and wrap. Refrigerate several hours or overnight. Slice dough ⅛ to ¼ inch thick. (Slice off only what you need, return unsliced dough to refrigerator and bake as needed. Dough will keep, covered, for a few weeks.) Place slices on ungreased cookie pans. Bake.

Oven Temperature: 375 degrees Fahrenheit.

Baking Time: about 10 minutes, or until golden brown.

Makes about 40 cookies.

* ½ cup of granulated and ½ cup of brown sugar may be used in place of all granulated sugar.

** ½ teaspoon almond extract or other flavoring may be used in place of the vanilla.

ORANGE REFRIGERATOR COOKIES

INGREDIENTS	METHOD
½ cup butter or margarine	*Cream well.*
1 cup granulated sugar	*Add gradually and mix well.*
1 egg 2 tblsps. grated orange rind	*Beat in, mix until thoroughly blended.*
2½ cups all-purpose flour 3 tsps. baking powder ¼ tsp. salt	*Sift together.*
¼ cup orange juice	*Add alternately with flour to egg mixture. Blend completely.*

SPECIAL INSTRUCTIONS: Divide dough in half and shape into 2 rolls on lightly floured board. Wrap in waxed paper and chill in refrigerator overnight or longer. Slice ⅛ inch thick, place on cookie pans. Bake.

Oven Temperature: 375 degrees Fahrenheit.

Baking Time: 10 to 12 minutes.

Makes about 60 cookies.

OLD-FASHIONED ICEBOX COOKIES

INGREDIENTS	METHOD
1 cup butter 1 cup granulated sugar	*Cream together.*
1 egg	*Beat in and cream for 2 minutes.*
2 cups all-purpose flour ¼ tsp. ground mace ½ tsp. powdered cinnamon ½ tsp. baking powder	*Sift together.*
½ cup pecan pieces ½ cup washed, drained and chopped seedless raisins	*Add to creamed mixture with flour mixture. Blend well.*

SPECIAL INSTRUCTIONS: Roll into long rolls and chill for several hours. Cut in about ⅛-inch-thick slices. Bake on lightly greased cookie pans.

Oven Temperature: 375 degrees Fahrenheit.

Baking Time: 8 to 10 minutes.

Makes about 64 cookies.

Tutti-Frutti Wheels

TUTTI-FRUTTI WHEELS

INGREDIENTS	METHOD
½ cup margarine	*Cream well.*
1 cup granulated sugar 1 egg beaten 1 tsp. almond extract	*Add and mix thoroughly.*
1½ cups cake flour ½ tsp. baking soda ¼ tsp. salt	*Sift together, add to egg mixture and blend.*
1 oz. (square) un- sweetened chocolate	*Melt over hot water and let cool. See instructions below.*
1 cup chopped, mixed candied fruit	*Use as described in instructions below.*

SPECIAL INSTRUCTIONS: Mix ⅓ of the dough with the melted and cooled chocolate. To the rest of the dough add the chopped fruit. Form into a roll. Refrigerate. Roll out the chocolate dough into a ⅛-inch-thick square. Brush with beaten egg white or water. Then place the chilled fruit roll at one end of the chocolate dough and roll the 2 together like a jelly roll. Refrigerate the double roll. Cut into thin slices with a thin sharp knife. Bake on cookie pans.

Oven Temperature: 375 degrees Fahrenheit.

Baking Time: about 10 minutes.

Makes about 60 cookies.

CHECKERBOARD SQUARES

INGREDIENTS	METHOD
1½ cups shortening	*Cream well.*
3 cups granulated sugar	*Add gradually to shortening and cream together.*
4 eggs	*Add 1 at a time, beat together.*
⅔ cup milk 1 tblsp. vanilla	*Add and blend, alternately with sifted dry ingredients.*
6 cups all-purpose flour 3 tsps. baking powder 1 tsp. salt	*Sift together, add as above. Blend thoroughly.*
Red pure-food coloring OR 2 oz. (squares) un- sweetened chocolate, melted over hot water 1 or 2 egg whites	*See instructions below.*

SPECIAL INSTRUCTIONS: Divide dough into 2 equal parts. Leave 1 part white. To the other add a few drops of red color, or the melted chocolate. Mix smoothly. Place the 2 doughs in the refrigerator to chill thoroughly. Roll ½ of the white dough on a lightly floured surface to a ½-inch-thick square. Brush top with lightly beaten egg white. Roll out ½ of the red (or chocolate) dough the same way to a square ½ inch thick. Place the red (or chocolate) square on top of the white square (which has the egg white on it). Repeat with the rest of the doughs so you have 4 layers, alternating the white and colored doughs. Return these 4 layers to the refrigerator. Chill.

Slice in ½-inch strips, brush with egg white. Reverse a strip, and lay the dark one on top of the strip covered with the egg white. Cover next white strip with a white strip, next white strip with a dark strip and you will have a 2-inch square with a checker-board design. Mix together and roll out the excess dough into a very thin square sheet. Brush with egg white, set the square checkerboard at the edge of it and cover the 4 sides of the checkerboard. Return to the refrigerator until thoroughly chilled. Cut into thin slices. Lay slices on cookie pans. Bake.

Oven Temperature: 400 degrees Fahrenheit.

Baking Time: 10 to 12 minutes.

NOTE: Any color combination, and 2-, 3- and 4-layer checker-boards can be made by the same plan.

Makes 7 or 8 dozen cookies.

MARBLE REFRIGERATOR COOKIES

INGREDIENTS	METHOD
1 cup butter 1 tsp. vanilla 1 cup sifted confectioners' sugar 1 tblsp. corn syrup	*Cream together. Add corn syrup.*
2½ cups all-purpose flour 1 tsp. salt Pure-food coloring	*Sift and blend in gradually. Add 2 or 3 tablespoons milk if needed for smooth stiff dough. See instructions below.*

SPECIAL INSTRUCTIONS: Divide dough into 4 parts. Color 1 part red, 1 yellow and 1 green by adding 4 drops of food coloring to each portion. Blend color in each dough thoroughly with a spoon or knead in with hands. Leave the 4th portion uncolored. Mix the 4 portions together carefully so each colored dough is mixed in but still distinctive. Do not beat to mix well. Make into rolls each 2 inches in diameter. Place in refrigerator to stiffen. When cold, cut with a sharp knife into ⅛-inch-thick slices. Place on cookie pans. Bake.

Oven Temperature: 375 degrees Fahrenheit.

Baking Time: 8 to 10 minutes.

Do not let cookies brown or they will lose the different colors which make them so attractive.

Makes about 5 dozen cookies.

NUT-REFRIGERATOR COOKIE SLICES

INGREDIENTS	METHOD
½ cup margarine	*Cream thoroughly.*
1 cup granulated sugar	*Add gradually and cream together.*
1 egg 1 tblsp. honey 1 tsp. almond extract	*Beat egg, blend in with honey and flavoring and mix well.*
2 cups all-purpose flour ½ tsp. baking soda ½ tsp. salt	*Sift together and add.*
½ cup shredded or finely chopped coconut ½ cup slivered almonds	*Add and mix thoroughly.*

SPECIAL INSTRUCTIONS: Press the mixture into a 9-inch square pan with 2-inch-high sides, the pan lined with waxed paper. Press dough evenly all around. Place in refrigerator until stiff. Remove from the pan and pull the paper off. Cut the 9-inch square of dough into strips about 2 inches wide. Then cut these in ⅛-inch slices. Place on greased cookie pans. Bake.

Oven Temperature: 375 degrees Fahrenheit.

Baking Time: 8 to 12 minutes.

NOTE: When covered, this dough may be kept in the refrigerator for a few weeks.

Makes about 64 cookies.

DATE-NUT REFRIGERATOR COOKIES

INGREDIENTS	METHOD
1 cup margarine	*Cream well.*
2 cups brown sugar 1 tsp. vanilla 1 tblsp. water 2 eggs, beaten	*Add, blend and mix until light.*
4 cups all-purpose flour ½ tsp. baking soda 1 tsp. salt	*Sift together.*
1 cup pitted dates, chopped ½ cup halved candied cherries 1 cup coarsely chopped nuts	*Mix with flour and add to egg mixture. Combine thoroughly.*

SPECIAL INSTRUCTIONS: Shape into 2 rolls or bars about 2 inches in diameter. Wrap in waxed paper and chill overnight. To bake slice in ⅛-inch pieces, place on greased cookie pans. Bake.

Oven Temperature: 375 degrees Fahrenheit.

Baking Time: 8 to 10 minutes.

When baked, remove at once from cookie pans and let cool on cake rack.

Makes about 8 dozen cookies.

Date-Nut Refrigerator Cookies

*An Assortment of
Refrigerator and
Tea Cookies*

MULTI-COLORED PINWHEELS

INGREDIENTS	METHOD
¾ cup shortening ½ cup granulated sugar ½ cup light brown sugar 2 eggs 1 tsp. vanilla	*Cream shortening and sugar together. Beat in eggs and flavoring.*
2½ cups all-purpose flour 1 tsp. baking powder 1 tsp. salt	*Sift together, mix into above until blended.*
2 oz. (squares) un-sweetened chocolate	*Melt over hot water, let cool slightly.*

SPECIAL INSTRUCTIONS: Divide dough in half. Blend melted chocolate into ½ of the dough. Chill. Roll remaining dough on a floured cloth into an oblong, 12 by 9 inches. Brush with water or slightly beaten egg white. Roll chocolate dough the same size; and place it on top of the white dough. Roll together until ³⁄₁₆ inch thick. Roll up tightly, beginning at wide side. Chill again. Cut in ⅛-inch-thick slices; place on ungreased cookie pans. Bake.

Oven Temperature: 375 degrees Fahrenheit.

Baking Time: 8 to 10 minutes.

Also, make different colored pinwheel cookies with this dough by adding pure-food coloring to it in place of the chocolate.

Makes 4 or 5 dozen cookies.

PRETZEL COOKIES

INGREDIENTS	METHOD
½ cup butter or shortening 1 cup sugar	*Cream together until light and fluffy.*
2 egg yolks	*Add and mix well.*
⅛ cup milk (2 tablespoons) 1½ cups flour 1 tsp. baking powder ⅛ tsp. baking soda ¼ tsp. salt ¼ tsp. ground mace	*Sift dry ingredients. Add alternately with milk to egg mixture. Blend.*

SPECIAL INSTRUCTIONS: Place in refrigerator to chill. Cut into small pieces. Roll each into 4- or 5-inch-long and ½-inch-thick strip. Shape each into a pretzel. Lay on greased cookie pans. Bake.

Oven Temperature: 375 degrees Fahrenheit.

Baking Time: 10 minutes, or until light brown color.

Cover top with melted chocolate or dust with confectioners' sugar.

Makes about 36 cookies.

23. SPRITZ COOKIES

BUTTER GEMS	
INGREDIENTS	METHOD
½ cup butter ½ cup shortening	*Cream well together.*
¾ cup sugar	*Add gradually.*
1 egg	*Add unbeaten and beat all together.*
2¼ cups all-purpose flour ½ tsp. baking powder Dash of salt 1 tsp. almond flavoring	*Sift flour, baking powder and salt together. Add with flavoring and blend thoroughly.*

SPECIAL INSTRUCTIONS: Form cookies with a cookie press onto ungreased pans. Bake.

Oven Temperature: 400 degrees Fahrenheit.

Baking Time: 10 to 12 minutes.

Makes about 60 cookies.

PLAIN SPRITZ COOKIES

INGREDIENTS	METHOD
½ cup margarine ½ cup butter 1 cup granulated sugar	*Cream together until light and fluffy.*
2 eggs	*Add 1 at a time, beat well.*
3 cups all-purpose flour	*Sift.*
½ tsp. vanilla	*Add with flour and mix until thoroughly blended.*

SPECIAL INSTRUCTIONS: Put dough in cookie press and press various shapes on lightly greased cookie pans. Bake.

Oven Temperature: 375 degrees Fahrenheit.

Baking Time: until the edges become a light brown in color.

Makes about 70 cookies.

CAT'S TONGUE cookies can be made with this dough. Press dough out as described, 2½ inches long and about the thickness of a pencil. Bake. When almost cool spread with melted bitter chocolate, or sweet chocolate, or leave plain.

CHOCOLATE LEAVES are made with the same dough. Squeeze thin layer of the spritz dough into metal or cardboard leaf cutouts. Remove cutouts, and repeat across cookie pans. Leave space between. Bake as described. Let cool. Cover thickly with melted bitter chocolate.

SPRITZ BUTTER COOKIES

INGREDIENTS	METHOD
½ cup butter ½ cup shortening	*Cream together until light.*
½ cup fine granulated sugar ¼ cup almond paste 1 egg, beaten	*Add and mix until smooth.*
½ tsp. vanilla 1 tblsp. rum flavoring 2 cups all-purpose flour	*Add flour gradually and mix thoroughly. Add flavorings.*

SPECIAL INSTRUCTIONS: Put mixture through cookie press into various shapes onto ungreased cookie pans. Bake.

Oven Temperature: 375 degrees Fahrenheit.

Baking Time: about 8 to 10 minutes.

NOTE: ¼ cup almond flour or ¼ cup almonds ground very fine may be substituted for the almond paste.

Makes about 50 cookies.

Chocolate Spritz Cookies

CHOCOLATE SPRITZ COOKIES

INGREDIENTS	METHOD
½ cup butter or margarine	*Cream well.*
1 cup granulated sugar 1 tsp. vanilla	*Add and cream together.*
1 egg	*Add and beat 1 minute.*
2 tblsps. milk	*Add and blend.*
2 cups cake flour ¼ tsp. salt	*Sift together and add,* *mixing until blended.*
2 oz. (squares) un- sweetened chocolate	*Melt over hot water, let* *cool. Add and blend well.*

SPECIAL INSTRUCTIONS: Form cookies with a cookie press onto ungreased cookie pans. Bake.

Oven Temperature: 375 degrees Fahrenheit.

Baking Time: 8 to 10 minutes.

NOTE: Spritz cookies can be shaped into any desired designs, such as daisies, scrolls, rosettes, or fingers. Use chocolate or vanilla icing to fill out the center of daisies.

Makes about 50 cookies.

SPRITZIES are made with this same dough. Use large star tube of pastry bag and form into bars on ungreased cookie pans. Bake at 400 degrees Fahrenheit for 8 to 10 minutes.

Makes about 3 dozen spritzies.

SPRITZ ROSETTES

INGREDIENTS	METHOD

½ cup shortening
½ cup peanut butter
    (creamy)
½ cup granulated sugar
½ cup brown sugar
¼ cup orange juice
  1 egg
	Beat together until very light and fluffy.

2 cups all-purpose flour ¼ tsp. salt ½ tsp. baking soda	*Sift together. Add to above and blend in until just mixed.*

SPECIAL INSTRUCTIONS: Using rosette or star plate in cookie press, form round cookies on ungreased cookie pans. Bake.

Oven Temperature: 350 degrees Fahrenheit.

Baking Time: 10 to 12 minutes.

Let cool on wire rack.

Makes 50 or more cookies.

VANILLA SPRITZ COOKIES

INGREDIENTS	METHOD
½ cup butter 1 cup granulated sugar	*Cream together thoroughly.*
2 eggs, beaten light 1 tblsp. light cream 1 tsp. vanilla	*Add and blend together.*
2¼ cups all-purpose flour ¼ tsp. baking powder ¼ tsp. salt ½ tsp. grated nutmeg	*Sift and add to above, mix well.*

SPECIAL INSTRUCTIONS: Squeeze cookies with press or star tube onto ungreased cookie pans. Bake.
Oven Temperature: 400 degrees Fahrenheit.
Baking Time: 8 to 10 minutes.
Makes about 54 cookies.

PECAN FINGER COOKIES

INGREDIENTS	METHOD
½ cup butter or margarine	*Cream thoroughly.*
⅓ cup confectioners' sugar	*Add and mix until smooth.*
1 egg yolk ¼ tsp. vanilla ½ tsp. almond extract	*Stir in.*
1½ cups cake flour	*Sift, add in several portions, mixing after each.*
½ cup finely ground pecans, extras for topping	*Add the ½ cup pecans and blend.*

SPECIAL INSTRUCTIONS: Use cookie press to shape small portions of dough into fingers about 2 inches long and ½ inch wide. Sprinkle with a few finely ground pecans. Bake.

Oven Temperature: 350 degrees Fahrenheit.

Baking Time: 10 to 15 minutes.

After slight cooling you may sprinkle baked fingers lightly with confectioners' sugar.

Makes 45 or more fingers.

ROYALTY COOKIES

INGREDIENTS	METHOD
½ cup butter or shortening ¼ cup granulated sugar	*Cream butter or shortening,* *add sugar gradually.*
2 egg yolks 1 tsp. lemon extract	*Add to above, continue* *creaming.*
1 cup all-purpose flour	*Add slowly, mix* *thoroughly.*

SPECIAL INSTRUCTIONS: Shape cookies on ungreased cookie pans with a cookie press. Bake.
Oven Temperature: 400 degrees Fahrenheit.
Baking Time: 8 to 10 minutes.
Makes about 24 cookies.

Pecan Finger
Cookies

SPRITZ DELIGHTS

INGREDIENTS	METHOD
1 cup butter or margarine ⅔ cup granulated sugar 3 egg yolks 1 tsp. vanilla or almond extract	*Mix thoroughly.*
2½ cups all-purpose flour	*Sift.*
¼ cup grated almonds	*Add with flour. Blend thoroughly.*

SPECIAL INSTRUCTIONS: Using ¼ of the dough at a time, force it through a cookie press onto an ungreased cookie pan in desired shapes. Bake.

Oven Temperature: 400 degrees Fahrenheit.

Baking Time: 7 to 10 minutes, or until done.

Makes about 54 cookies.

CHOCOLATE SPRITZ DELIGHTS: Make Spritz Delights as above but blend 2 squares (2 ounces) melted unsweetened chocolate into the shortening mixture. Complete the recipe as above.

SOUR-CREAM COOKIES

INGREDIENTS	METHOD
1 cup shortening	*Cream well.*
1 cup granulated sugar	*Add and mix well.*
2 egg yolks, beaten ½ cup thick sour cream (commercial) 1 tsp. vanilla	*Add and mix in.*
4 cups all-purpose flour ½ tsp. salt 1 tsp. grated nutmeg ½ tsp. baking soda	*Sift together, gradually add to the above. Mix well after each addition.*

SPECIAL INSTRUCTIONS: Form dough in desired shapes on ungreased cookie pans using a cookie press. Bake.

Oven Temperature: 400 degrees Fahrenheit.

Baking Time: 10 to 12 minutes.

Makes about 8 or 9 dozen.

SPRITZ DAISIES

INGREDIENTS	METHOD
1 cup shortening	*Beat until soft.*
¾ cup granulated sugar	*Add and cream until light.*
1 egg 1 tsp. vanilla	*Add and mix until smooth.*
2¾ cups all-purpose flour ¼ tsp. salt ½ tsp. baking powder	*Sift together. Add and blend thoroughly.*

SPECIAL INSTRUCTIONS: Shape with a cookie press, or large star tube pastry bag, into daisies. Fill center of each with a little raspberry jam. Bake.

Oven Temperature: 375 degrees Fahrenheit.

Baking Time: 12 to 15 minutes.

Makes about 56 cookies.

Swedish Supreme Cookies

SWEDISH SUPREME COOKIES

INGREDIENTS	METHOD
½ cup margarine ½ cup butter	*Cream together until smooth.*
½ cup fine granulated sugar	*Add and mix well.*
½ tsp. vanilla 4 egg yolks	*Add gradually, mixing continuously until fluffy.*
1 tsp. salt ⅛ tsp. baking soda 2¼ cups all-purpose flour	*Sift together, add and blend until well mixed.*

SPECIAL INSTRUCTIONS: Press through a cookie press or pastry bag and tube onto ungreased cookie pans. Bake.

Oven Temperature: 375 degrees Fahrenheit.

Baking Time: 10 to 12 minutes.

NOTE: This mixture also may be chilled, then rolled out on a well floured board and cut into various shapes using small cutters. When baked, set 2 cookies together with jam. Dip some of the cookies into melted and cooled Bittersweet Chocolate Frosting (Page 291).

Makes about 36 cookies.

24. SUGAR COOKIES

DAINTY SUGAR COOKIES

INGREDIENTS	METHOD
1 cup butter 1½ cups granulated sugar	*Cream together.*
2 eggs beaten 5 tblsps. milk	*Add and blend in.*
3 cups all-purpose flour 1 tsp. baking powder	*Sift together. Add to above and mix until dough is smooth.*

SPECIAL INSTRUCTIONS: Roll out into ⅛-inch thickness on a floured board or pastry cloth. Cut with 1-inch or 1½-inch cookie cutters. Brush with a mixture of 1 egg, pinch of salt and 2 tablespoons milk. Or use milk alone. Place on ungreased cookie pans. Sprinkle with regular or coarse granulated sugar. Bake.

Oven Temperature: 375 degrees Fahrenheit.

Baking Time: about 6 to 8 minutes.

Makes 10 to 12 dozen cookies.

CRESCENT SUGAR COOKIES

INGREDIENTS	METHOD
½ cup butter	*Cream.*
1 cup granulated sugar 1 egg OR 2 egg yolks 1 tblsp. cream or milk ½ tsp. vanilla	*Beat in and blend well.*
1½ cups all-purpose flour ¼ tsp. salt 1 tsp. baking powder	*Sift together, add to creamed mixture and blend.*
½ cup washed, drained chopped seedless raisins ¼ cup chopped nuts	*Stir in.*

SPECIAL INSTRUCTIONS: Place dough in refrigerator for about 2 hours. Shape small amounts into individual crescents. Or roll out and cut with crescent cutter. Place them on greased cookie sheets, 1 inch apart. Bake.

Oven Temperature: 375 degrees Fahrenheit.

Baking Time: about 8 minutes.

To emphasize the butter flavor, brush the cookies lightly with melted butter while they are still warm. After the crescents have cooled slightly, sprinkle with sifted confectioners' sugar.

Makes about 50 cookies.

COUNTRY SUGAR COOKIES

INGREDIENTS	METHOD
1 cup butter ¾ cup granulated sugar	*Cream together for 5 minutes.*
1 egg 1 tblsp. grated lemon rind 2 tblsps. lemon juice	*Add and blend.*
2½ cups all-purpose flour 1½ tsps. baking powder ⅛ tsp. salt	*Sift together.*
½ cup milk	*Add with flour mixture to egg and sugar, mix until smooth.*

SPECIAL INSTRUCTIONS: Chill dough for at least 1 hour. Roll about ½ of dough out on a floured board to ⅛-inch thickness. Brush with mixture of 1 egg, pinch of salt and 2 tablespoons milk. Sprinkle with granulated sugar. Cut with plain or scalloped cookie cutter. Place cookies on lightly greased cookie pans. Bake.

Oven Temperature: 375 degrees Fahrenheit.

Baking Time: 10 to 12 minutes.

Roll out rest of dough and cut cookies as described. Bake a few at a time.

Makes about 3 dozen cookies.

DECORATED SUGAR COOKIES

INGREDIENTS	METHOD
1 cup butter or margarine	*Cream.*
2 cups granulated sugar	*Add gradually and cream together.*
2 eggs, beaten 1 tsp. vanilla 1 tsp. lemon extract 2 tblsps. milk or cream	*Add, beat until smooth and creamy.*
3½ cups all-purpose flour 2 tsps. baking powder 1 tsp. salt	*Sift together. Blend into the above, mixing in a small amount at a time.*

FOR DECORATIONS: 1 egg white, colored sugar, sugar-and-cinnamon, tiny colored candies, chopped candied cherries, citron, chopped nuts or halves, etc.

SPECIAL INSTRUCTIONS: Chill dough, roll thin and cut with holiday type or other cookie cutters. Place on greased cookie pans. Brush with slightly beaten egg white and sprinkle with decorations. Bake.

Oven Temperature: 350 degrees Fahrenheit.

Baking Time: 10 to 12 minutes until delicately browned.

Makes about 70 cookies.

GRANNY'S SUGAR COOKIES

INGREDIENTS	METHOD
½ cup butter ½ cup shortening 1 cup granulated sugar	*Cream together.*
3 eggs beaten	*Add and blend well.*
3½ cups all-purpose flour 1 tsp. baking soda 2 tsps. cream of tartar	*Sift together, add gradually to above and mix.*
1½ tsps. vanilla	*Add and blend well.*

SPECIAL INSTRUCTIONS: Chill the dough. Roll out on floured pastry cloth to ¼-inch thickness. Cut with 2½-inch round cookie cutter. Brush lightly with milk, water or slightly beaten egg white. Sprinkle with sugar. Bake.

Oven Temperature: 425 degrees Fahrenheit.

Baking Time: 6 to 8 minutes.

Makes about 40 cookies.

SOUTHERN SUGAR COOKIES

INGREDIENTS	METHOD
½ cup butter or shortening	*Cream thoroughly.*
1 cup granulated sugar 1 egg, beaten 1 tsp. grated lemon rind 1 tblsp. lemon juice	*Add and mix together.*
½ tsp. baking soda ½ cup sour milk	*Add soda to milk, mix well.* *Add to above alternately* *with flour mixture.*
3½ cups all-purpose flour 1 tsp. baking powder ¼ tsp. salt	*Sift together, add as* *described to make a* *medium stiff dough.*

SPECIAL INSTRUCTIONS: Roll out very thin on floured cloth or board and cut with round, fluted cookie cutter. Brush cookies with milk; sprinkle with sugar. Place on ungreased cookie pans and bake. Or add ground pecans and raisins to sugar, sprinkle, and bake.

Oven Temperature: 375 degrees Fahrenheit.

Baking Time: about 10 minutes.

Makes about 50 cookies.

VARIATION: Roll small portions of dough at a time, very thin. Cut with 3¼-inch round cutter. Place on ungreased cookie pans. Sprinkle with sugar. Bake at 400 degrees Fahrenheit.

Makes about 40 large cookies.

FILLED SUGAR COOKIES

INGREDIENTS	METHOD
½ cup margarine	*Cream well.*
1 cup granulated sugar	*Add gradually and cream together until light.*
1 egg well beaten 1 tblsp. milk or cream 1 tsp. vanilla	*Add to above.*
1½ cups all-purpose flour 1½ tsps. baking powder ½ tsp. salt	*Sift together, add gradually to above, beating well.*
½ cup all-purpose flour	*Add until dough is stiff enough to handle.*

SPECIAL INSTRUCTIONS: Chill at least 1 hour. Roll dough on floured board to ⅛-inch thickness. Cut with medium sized round or square cookie cutter. Place cookies on lightly greased cookie pans, then place ½ teaspoon of filling, such as strawberry, raspberry, fig or pineapple jam in the center of the cookies. Cover each with a plain cookie the same size and shape. Press edges of cookies together with tines of a fork dipped in flour. Bake.

Oven Temperature: 375 degrees Fahrenheit.

Baking Time: 8 to 10 minutes.

Remove from pans at once onto cake rack to cool.

VARIATION NO. 1: Prepare recipe as above and bake cookies without filling. When cool, spread a little filling on half the cookies and cover with remaining cookies to make "sandwiches."

VARIATION NO. 2: Prepare recipe for the dough. Roll out and cut into squares. Add a little filling to each cookie and fold over diagonally to make a triangle. Seal triangles by pressing edges together. Bake as above.

Makes about 20 filled cookies or sandwich cookies. Or 40 triangles.

SUGAR GEMS

INGREDIENTS	METHOD
1 cup butter or shortening	*Cream well.*
2 cups granulated sugar	*Add and cream together.*
4 egg yolks	*Add and blend well.*
¼ cup milk	*Add and mix.*
2 tsps. baking powder ¼ tsp. baking soda ½ tsp. salt 1 tsp. ground mace 3½ cups all-purpose flour	*Sift together and beat gradually into the above.*

SPECIAL INSTRUCTIONS: Chill the mixture in the refrigerator. If you want to bake without chilling, roll small portions of dough in your fingers into small balls. Place on cookie pan 2 to 3 inches apart to allow spread of dough. Or roll chilled dough on floured board, to about ⅛-inch thickness. Cut with cookie cutter. Bake.

Oven Temperature: 375 degrees Fahrenheit.

Baking Time: 12 to 15 minutes.

Makes 60 rolled cookies, 70 or more ball cookies.

SCOTCH SHORTBREAD COOKIES

INGREDIENTS	METHOD
1 cup butter	*Cream thoroughly.*
1 tsp. vanilla or ½ tsp. lemon extract	*Blend in.*
½ cup confectioners' sugar	*Add gradually, cream together until light and fluffy.*
2 cups all-purpose flour	*Mix in gradually and work with your hands to make smooth dough.*

SPECIAL INSTRUCTIONS: Press or roll dough to ½-inch-thick rectangle. Prick in several places with fork, or press any design you like on top. Cut in 1-inch squares or other shapes. Place on ungreased cookie pans. Bake.

Oven Temperature: 375 degrees Fahrenheit.

Baking Time: 15 minutes.

Let cool on cake racks.

Makes 24 or more pieces shortbread.

25. VANILLA COOKIES

VANILLA SCROLL COOKIES

INGREDIENTS	METHOD
⅔ cup butter 1 cup sugar	*Cream well together.*
3 eggs	*Add 1 at a time, beating in well.*
1 tsp. vanilla 4 cups all-purpose flour ½ tsp. salt	*Add vanilla, and flour sifted with salt. Mix into smooth dough.*

SPECIAL INSTRUCTIONS: Refrigerate. To bake make small balls of dough about the size of a walnut. Roll each out by hand lightly and form into a ¼-inch-thick strip. Shape these into scrolls, rings, hearts, oblongs, letters, etc., on a lightly floured baking pan. Bake.

Oven Temperature: 375 degrees Fahrenheit.

Baking Time: about 10 minutes.

Makes 50 or 60 scroll cookies.

VANILLA DAISIES

INGREDIENTS	METHOD
½ cup butter ½ cup shortening ¼ tsp. salt	*Cream together well.*
⅔ cup granulated sugar	*Add slowly, beating together.*
1 egg, beaten	*Add and mix well.*
1 tsp. vanilla 1 tsp. fresh grated lemon rind	*Add and mix in.*
2¼ cups all-purpose flour ½ tsp. baking powder	*Sift flour and baking powder together. Add, mix thoroughly, but do not over-mix.*

SPECIAL INSTRUCTIONS: Press dough through a cookie press, or pastry bag using No. 5 star tube. Place a candied cherry half or a little raspberry jam in the center of each cookie. Bake.

Oven Temperature: 375 degrees Fahrenheit.

Baking Time: 8 to 10 minutes.

Makes 40 or more cookies.

*Vanilla
Daisies*

*Vanilla
Sour-Cream
Rosettes*

VANILLA SOUR-CREAM ROSETTES

INGREDIENTS	METHOD
¼ cup butter ¼ cup shortening ½ cup sugar	*Cream well together.*
1 egg	*Add and beat until mixture is light.*
¼ cup sour cream (commercial) ½ tsp. vanilla	*Stir in.*
1½ cups all-purpose flour ½ tsp. powdered cinnamon ¼ tsp. salt ⅛ tsp. baking soda ½ tsp. baking powder	*Sift together, add to cream mixture and mix thoroughly.*

SPECIAL INSTRUCTIONS: Force dough through pastry bag or cookie press into rosettes onto ungreased cookie pans. Bake.

Oven Temperature: 375 degrees Fahrenheit.

Baking Time: 10 to 12 minutes.

Makes 48 or more rosettes.

26. WALNUT COOKIES

WALNUT CRESCENTS

INGREDIENTS	METHOD
1 cup butter or margarine ¼ cup confectioners' sugar	*Have butter or margarine at room temperature. Cream with sugar 5 minutes.*
2 cups all-purpose flour 1½ tsps. water 2 tsps. vanilla 1 cup finely chopped walnuts ½ tsp. almond extract	*Add flour and mix well. Stir in water, flavorings and nuts.*

SPECIAL INSTRUCTIONS: Chill dough about ½ hour. Shape into rolls about ½ inch in diameter. Cut in 1-inch pieces. Roll each 1-inch piece in your fingers into 2½-inch-long piece. Place on cookie pans and pull ends down slightly to form crescent shape. Bake.

Oven Temperature: 375 degrees Fahrenheit.

Baking Time: 12 to 15 minutes.

Let cool. Roll in confectioners' sugar.

Makes about 4 dozen crescents.

WALNUT ROCKS

INGREDIENTS	METHOD
1 cup butter or margarine	*Cream well.*
1 cup sugar	*Add and mix until smooth.*
4 egg yolks	*Beat in 1 at a time.*
2¼ cups all-purpose flour 1 tsp. powdered cinnamon 1 tsp. ground cloves	*Sift together.*
1 cup finely chopped walnuts 1½ cups washed and drained seedless raisins	*Add to flour and stir into creamed mixture, mixing well.*
1 tsp. baking soda 1½ tsps. boiling water	*Add soda to water, stir into batter.*
4 egg whites	*Beat until stiff, fold into batter.*

SPECIAL INSTRUCTIONS: Drop from teaspoon onto lightly floured cookie pans. Bake.

Oven Temperature: 350 degrees Fahrenheit.

Baking Time: 15 to 18 minutes or until done.

Makes 8 or 9 dozen.

WALNUT BUTTERBALLS

INGREDIENTS	METHOD
½ cup butter or margarine	*Beat until creamy.*
2 tblsps. honey	*Stir in.*
1 cup sifted all-purpose flour ¼ tsp. salt 1 tsp. vanilla 1 cup finely chopped walnuts	*Add and mix thoroughly.*
Confectioners' sugar	*Use as described in instructions below.*

SPECIAL INSTRUCTIONS: Chill dough 1 hour. To bake, form into balls the size of walnuts. Place 2 inches apart on greased baking sheets. Bake.

Oven Temperature: 300 degrees Fahrenheit.

Baking Time: 35 minutes, or until delicately browned.

Roll hot cookies in confectioners' sugar. Let cool and roll in sugar again.

Makes about 2 dozen cookies.

BROWN WALNUT COOKIES

INGREDIENTS	METHOD
⅔ cup margarine 2 cups brown sugar	*Cream together.*
2 eggs, beaten	*Add and beat 3 minutes.*
⅔ cup sour milk 1 tsp. vanilla	*Add and blend well, alternately with flour mixture.*
3 cups all-purpose flour 1 tsp. baking powder ½ tsp. baking soda 1 tsp. salt ½ tsp. powdered cinnamon	*Sift together, and combine smoothly as described.*
1 cup finely chopped walnuts	*Add and mix well.*

SPECIAL INSTRUCTIONS: Drop by teaspoon onto lightly greased cookie pans. Leave 2 inches between cookies. Bake.
Oven Temperature: 350 degrees Fahrenheit.
Baking Time: about 10 minutes.
Makes about 7 dozen cookies.

ENGLISH-WALNUT COOKIES

INGREDIENTS	METHOD
½ cup light brown sugar ½ cup shortening ½ cup butter ⅛ tsp. salt ½ tsp. almond extract ½ tsp. vanilla	*Cream together lightly.*
1 egg, beaten	*Add to above and blend.*
2 cups all-purpose flour	*Sift.*
¾ cup finely chopped English walnuts	*Mix with flour and add to egg mixture. Blend well.*

SPECIAL INSTRUCTIONS: Chill dough in refrigerator for about 30 minutes. Roll out on floured cloth to ⅛-inch thickness, or the thickness of chopped walnuts. Cut out with a 3-inch round cookie cutter. Place on lightly greased cookie pans, brush top with a mixture of 1 beaten egg, 2 tablespoons milk and a pinch of salt. Place a half walnut on the center of each cookie. Bake.

Oven Temperature: 350 degrees Fahrenheit.

Baking Time: about 15 minutes.

Makes about 3 dozen cookies.

WALNUT DROPS

INGREDIENTS	METHOD
½ cup soft margarine ¼ cup brown sugar	*Cream together well.*
1 egg	*Add and beat 5 minutes.*
1 tblsp. milk 1½ tsps. grated orange rind ½ tsp. lemon extract	*Blend in.*
1 cup all-purpose flour ¼ tsp. salt	*Sift together, add to above and mix until thoroughly incorporated.*
¾ cup finely chopped walnuts	

SPECIAL INSTRUCTIONS: Refrigerate dough for about 1 hour. To bake make into small balls and roll in the finely chopped walnuts. Bake on ungreased cookie pans.

Oven Temperature: 350 degrees Fahrenheit.

Baking Time: 12 to 15 minutes.

Makes about 2 dozen balls.

FILLINGS, ICINGS
AND FROSTINGS

27. FILLINGS FOR COOKIES

SPECIAL FIG FILLING

INGREDIENTS	METHOD
1½ cups dried figs	*Cover figs with boiling water, let stand 10 to 15 minutes. Drain, clip off stems and cut fine using scissors.*
1 cup cold water	*Add and cook until tender, about 10 to 12 minutes.*
½ cup corn syrup 1 tsp. grated lemon rind	*Add and cook a few minutes longer.*
6 tblsps. granulated sugar 2 tblsps. cornstarch ¹⁄₁₆ tblsp. salt	*Mix together, add to figs all at once. Cook, while stirring, until thickened and clear. Remove from heat.*
1 tblsp. lemon juice ½ cup chopped nuts	*Add and let cool.*

Makes about 2 cups filling.

FIG FILLING

INGREDIENTS	METHOD
2 cups (1 lb.) fresh figs	*Cut in small pieces. Or soak dried figs 1 hour, then drain. Clip off stems. Cut fine.*
½ cup water ½ cup granulated sugar	*Add to above in double boiler. Cook 10 to 12 minutes, stirring frequently.*
1 cup finely chopped pecans	*Add and let cool.*

Makes about 3 cups filling.

DATE-PEANUT BUTTER FILLING

INGREDIENTS	METHOD
1 cup pitted dates, cut up ⅔ cup water ¼ cup granulated sugar ¹⁄₁₆ tsp. salt	*Combine in saucepan and cook over medium heat, stirring constantly, until thick. Let cool.*
2 tblsps. peanut butter	*Stir in and blend well.*

Makes about 1½ cups filling.

28. ICINGS AND FROSTINGS
(BOTTOMS, COATINGS, TOPPINGS, WHIPS)

BUTTER-CREAM ICING

INGREDIENTS	METHOD
3 tblsps. margarine or butter	*Have at room temperature. Beat until creamy.*
1½ cups confectioners' sugar	*Sift.*
3 or more tsps. light cream	*Add alternately with the sifted sugar to creamed butter until right consistency.*
½ tsp. vanilla Pinch of salt	*Add and beat until fluffy.*

Makes about 2 cups icing.

FONDANT ICING	
INGREDIENTS	METHOD
1 cup water 1 cup granulated sugar ⅓ cup white corn syrup	*Combine and bring to a boil.*

Sifted confectioners' sugar,
    add as needed
    (5 to 6 cups)
	Stir in immediately, and continue until smooth.

Pure-food coloring	*Add a few drops coloring and mix until the shade of icing you desire has been obtained.*

SPECIAL INSTRUCTIONS: While it is still warm, pour this icing over the Petits Fours which have been placed on a cookie rack. If the icing becomes cool and stiff, heat in a double boiler over hot water adding a little hot water and mixing.

To make CHOCOLATE FONDANT ICING, scrape all the different colored icings together which have dripped down into the pan under the rack. Heat them in a double boiler over hot water and add 4 tablespoons hot water and 2 squares (2 ounces) unsweetened chocolate, melted, to the icing. Stir until well blended and soft enough to pour over Petits Fours. This should be done immediately, while icing is hot.

Makes about 3 cups icing.

GLOSSY CHOCOLATE FROSTING

INGREDIENTS	METHOD
½ cup semi-sweet chocolate bits 2 tblsps. confectioners' sugar 2 tblsps. water ½ tsp. rum flavoring	*Melt chocolate over hot water. Combine all ingredients in top of double boiler, stir well to blend. Do not boil.*

SPECIAL INSTRUCTIONS: Reheat if the frosting becomes too thick and stiff.

Makes about ¾ cup frosting.

BITTERSWEET CHOCOLATE FROSTING

SPECIAL INSTRUCTIONS: Use any amount of bittersweet chocolate and melt slowly in a double boiler over hot water, while stirring occasionally. After it is melted, let cool to 86 degrees Fahrenheit. This coating used on cookies and petits fours will set immediately in a cool place, or when placed in the refrigerator for a few minutes. Use on Cat's Tongues and Chocolate Leaves.

CHOCOLATE ICING

INGREDIENTS	METHOD
1 oz. (square) unsweetened chocolate	*Melt over hot water. Remove from heat, let cool.*
2 tblsps. butter 2 tblsps. light cream 1 cup sifted confectioners' sugar 1 tsp. vanilla	*Combine, beat until smooth, and add cooled chocolate. Beat well.*

SPECIAL INSTRUCTIONS: Use to frost Hawaiian Brownies. For BITTER CHOCOLATE ICING, use bitter chocolate in this recipe.

Makes about 1¼ cups icing.

QUICK CHOCOLATE TOPPINGS

INGREDIENTS	METHOD
1 cup semi-sweet chocolate bits 1 tblsp. shortening	*Melt chocolate over hot water. Blend with shortening.*

NOTE: For quick bittersweet chocolate topping use 1 cup bittersweet chocolate cut fine. Melt as described, but combine with 3 tablespoons lukewarm milk instead of shortening. Or omit milk. Stir chocolate with wooden spoon until the chocolate reaches 86 degrees Fahrenheit on a candy thermometer. Test a little on waxed paper to see if the chocolate is cool enough to cover the cookie and not run off the edges. Spread on cookies. Cool the chocolate on the cookies by placing them in the refrigerator for a few minutes.

Makes about 1 cup.

CHOCOLATE FROSTING

INGREDIENTS	METHOD
2 oz. (squares) unsweetened chocolate	*Melt over hot water.*
15-oz. can sweetened condensed milk	*Add. Stir and beat as mixture begins to thicken. Continue beating until of spreading consistency. Remove from heat and from the hot water.*
1 tsp. vanilla Pinch of salt	*Stir in.*

SPECIAL INSTRUCTIONS: Use immediately, while still warm. Best for cooled brownies while they are still in pan and uncut.

Makes about 1½ cups.

CONFECTIONERS' ICING

INGREDIENTS	METHOD
1 egg white 1 to 1½ cups sifted confectioners' sugar ½ tsp. cream of tartar	*Heat to lukewarm (90 degrees Fahrenheit) in a double boiler over hot water and then beat until it stands in peaks. Use at once.*

SPECIAL INSTRUCTIONS: If this icing must stand, cover with a damp cloth. This prevents a crust forming.

TO COLOR THIS ICING use pure-food coloring. For a stiffer icing, add a little more confectioners' sugar.

VARIATION: Combine 2½ cups confectioners' sugar, 1 tablespoon white corn syrup, 2 tablespoons butter, and 3 to 4 tablespoons hot water. Beat until blended and smooth.

Makes about 2½ cups icing.

RICH BUTTER-CREAM FROSTING

INGREDIENTS	METHOD
½ cup butter or margarine 1½ cups sifted confectioners' sugar	*Cream together until light and fluffy.*
1 tsp. vanilla Pinch of salt	*Add and blend.*
1 egg white	*Add unbeaten and continue beating or whipping until fluffy.*

NOTE: This frosting can be used for frosting cake, and for making flowers, leaves, etc. as decorations on the cake.

Makes about 2½ cups frosting.

DECORATING ICING I

INGREDIENTS	METHOD
2¼ cups sifted confectioners' sugar 2 egg whites ¼ tsp. cream of tartar	*Heat all ingredients to luke-warm in double boiler. Remove from heat. Beat in electric mixer at high speed for 5 or 6 minutes until icing stands in peaks.*

SPECIAL INSTRUCTIONS: Or use electric mixer and beat at high speed about 5 or 6 minutes until icing holds a point. Cover bowl with a damp cloth until you are ready to use the icing. Tint as you wish and decorate cookies or Petits Fours, using pastry bag and decorating tube. Also called ROYAL ICING.

Makes about 2¾ cups icing.

DECORATING ICING II

INGREDIENTS	METHOD
2 cups sifted confectioners' sugar 1 egg white, stiffly beaten ¼ tsp. vanilla	*Mix until thoroughly blended.*
1½ tblsps. or more hot milk or cream	*Add very small amount to sugar mixture until a stiff paste results. Cream well. Add a few more drops of milk until proper consistency for decorating.*
Pure-food coloring	*Add a drop or two at a time until desired shade is obtained.*

SPECIAL INSTRUCTIONS: Icing will crust easily, so keep covered with damp cloth when not using. Spread icing on cookies with spatula or pastry brush. Try lemon, almond or peppermint flavorings for variety.

Makes about 2 cups icing.

MAPLE-NUT ICING

INGREDIENTS	METHOD
1 tblsp. white corn syrup 2 tblsps. maple-nut flavoring 2 tblsps. water	*Heat together until quite warm. Do not boil.*
3 to 3½ cups sifted confectioners' sugar (variable)	*Beat in enough sugar to make a fairly stiff icing. Beat until smooth.*

SPECIAL INSTRUCTIONS: Put icing on cookies while it is still warm so it will harden and dry on the cookies.

Makes about 3¼ cups icing.

PEANUT-BUTTER TOPPING

INGREDIENTS	METHOD
½ cup peanut butter 1 tblsp. cream	*Heat in top of double boiler over hot water. Stir to blend well. Do not boil. When blended spread on cookies. Let dry.*

Makes about ½ cup topping.

GLAZE ICING

INGREDIENTS	METHOD
½ cup granulated sugar ¼ cup water	*Boil together until it threads from the spoon (230 degrees Fahrenheit). Remove from heat.*

Confectioners' sugar
    (approximately
    ¼ cup)
	Stir in confectioners' sugar to make right consistency.

SPECIAL INSTRUCTIONS: Brush hot icing lightly over cookies. Also called WHITE ICING GLAZE when 1 teaspoon cornstarch is sifted with the confectioners' sugar. Brush while hot over lebkuchen.

Makes about 1 cup icing.

CONFECTIONERS' CREAM ICING

INGREDIENTS	METHOD
2 tblsps. butter 1 cup confectioners' sugar (variable)	*Cream together.*
2 tblsps. cream ¼ tsp. vanilla	*Add and mix completely.*

SPECIAL INSTRUCTIONS: More sugar may be added, if necessary, to obtain spreading consistency. For RUM ICING, use 1 teaspoon rum flavoring in place of vanilla.

Makes about 1¼ cups icing.

PECAN FROSTING

INGREDIENTS	METHOD
¼ cup butter 2 cups confectioners' sugar 1 tblsp. light molasses	*Cream together until well blended and smooth.*
¼ cup chopped pecans	*Stir in.*
2 tblsps. light cream (variable)	*Add gradually until frosting is of spreading consistency.*

Makes about 2¾ cups frosting.

SUGAR GLAZE

INGREDIENTS	METHOD
¾ cup sifted confectioners' sugar ½ tsp. vanilla 3 to 4 tsps. hot water	*Mix together until smooth and of frosting consistency. Add a few extra drops hot water if needed.*
Food coloring, if desired	

SPECIAL INSTRUCTIONS: This glaze is a nice thin icing for lebkuchen, cookies, French doughnuts, Danish pastries, etc.
Makes about 1 cup.

LEMON CONFECTIONERS' SUGAR ICING

INGREDIENTS	METHOD
1 cup water 4 tblsps. lemon juice ¼ cup cornstarch	*Cook until thickened, stirring constantly.*
1 tblsp. melted butter 1 tsp. lemon extract 3 drops yellow pure-food coloring	*Add and blend.*
1¾ cups sifted confectioners' sugar	*Add sugar gradually and stir until thick.*

SPECIAL INSTRUCTIONS: Set icing in top of double boiler over hot water to keep warm and spreadable.

Makes about 3 cups icing.

PINEAPPLE ICING

INGREDIENTS	METHOD
½ cup pineapple juice ½ cup water ¼ cup cornstarch	*Mix until smooth, cook over medium heat, stirring constantly until thickened. Remove from heat.*
1 tblsp. lemon juice 1 tblsp. orange juice 3 tblsps. butter, melted 1 tsp. vanilla 2 drops yellow pure- food coloring	*Add and mix until blended.*
1¾ cups sifted confectioners' sugar	*Add and mix until thoroughly blended.*

Makes 3¾ cups icing.

FANCY ORANGE ICING

INGREDIENTS	METHOD
1½ cups sifted confectioners' sugar 1 tsp. butter at room temperature 2½ tblsps. orange juice 1 tsp. grated orange rind	*Combine all ingredients. Beat until smooth.*

SPECIAL INSTRUCTIONS: Mix until well blended. The grated rind may be omitted for PLAIN ORANGE ICING. For another delicious ORANGE FROSTING use ¼ cup orange juice and enough confectioners' sugar to make a smooth thick icing. Beat in 1 teaspoon melted butter. Use at once.

Makes about 1¼ cups icing.

SIMPLE SYRUP

INGREDIENTS	METHOD
4 tblsps. granulated sugar 4 tblsps. water 2 tblsps. white corn syrup	*Bring to a boil.*

SPECIAL INSTRUCTIONS: Follow recipe instructions and apply with pastry brush to cookies while they are still hot.

Makes about ½ cup.

LEMON ICING

INGREDIENTS	METHOD
1 cup sifted confectioners' sugar 2 tblsps. fresh lemon juice	*Mix together until smooth. Add more lemon juice if needed.*
⅓ cup finely chopped walnuts	*See instructions.*

SPECIAL INSTRUCTIONS: Dip both ends of baked Chocolate Dips in this icing about ¼ inch up and then dip the icing-covered ends into the chopped or ground walnuts. Let dry on waxed paper.

Makes about 1 cup icing.

COLORED SUGAR

INGREDIENTS	METHOD
1 cup granulated sugar Red, green or yellow pure-food coloring	*Mix together, add 1 or 2 drops of one color until sugar has taken the color evenly.*

SPECIAL INSTRUCTIONS: Spread colored sugar on pan covered with waxed paper. Allow to dry for a few minutes. Put through coarse sieve or rub between your fingers and the sugar is ready to use.

LEMON SUGAR. Mix 1 teaspoon finely grated lemon peel with ¼ cup sugar.

CARAMEL ICING

INGREDIENTS	METHOD
1 cup brown sugar ¼ cup milk	*Combine in saucepan; let come to a boil over low heat. Boil 5 minutes, stirring constantly.*
3 tblsps. butter	*Add and mix enough to blend. Remove from heat.*
3 cups confectioners' sugar	*Add the brown sugar-butter-and-milk mixture to the confectioners' sugar. Mix smoothly.*
1 tblsp. concentrated maple flavoring	*Add and blend well.*

SPECIAL INSTRUCTIONS: If the icing is too thick, stir in a little more milk until desired consistency.

Makes about 4 cups icing.

STRAWBERRY WHIP

INGREDIENTS	METHOD
3 cups granulated sugar 1 egg white 1 tblsp. lemon juice 1 pint fresh strawberries	*Whip sugar and egg white into a stiff meringue. Combine all in an electric mixer. Chill.*

SPECIAL INSTRUCTIONS: Fill meringue shells or use as a filling for "hollows" and topping for cake.

NOTE: ½ teaspoon plain gelatin, soaked in 1 tablespoon cold water for 5 minutes, then dissolved over hot water until clear, if added to the strawberry mixture while beating, will give it a little more stability.

Makes 3 or more cups.

STRAWBERRY WHIPPED CREAM

INGREDIENTS	METHOD
1 cup cold whipping cream	*Whip until thick.*
1 tblsp. sifted confectioners' sugar	*Add and blend.*
⅓ cup or more fresh strawberries	*Chop and fold into cream.*

Makes over 2 cups.

PLAIN COOKIE DOUGH FOR COOKIE BOTTOMS

INGREDIENTS	METHOD
1 cup shortening ¼ cup granulated sugar	*Have shortening at room temperature. Combine with sugar beating until smooth.*
2 eggs, beaten 1 tsp. vanilla	*Add and blend.*
2 cups all-purpose flour ½ tsp. salt ¼ tsp. baking powder	*Sift together. Mix only until blended.*

SPECIAL INSTRUCTIONS: Use dough for bottom of slices, etc. as requested in various recipes.

STREUSSEL

INGREDIENTS	METHOD
½ cup butter	*Cream.*
½ cup granulated sugar	*Add gradually and cream well.*
1 tsp. grated lemon rind 1 tsp. powdered cinnamon 1¾ cups sifted all-purpose flour	*Add; mix with fingers until well mixed and crumbly.*

SPECIAL INSTRUCTIONS: Streussel may be pressed through a coarse sieve to obtain more uniform crumbs.

Makes about 2¼ cups.

IMITATION PISTACHIO NUTS

INGREDIENTS	METHOD
½ cup grated or chopped coconut 2 drops green pure-food coloring 1 drop yellow pure-food coloring	*Mix together well.*

SPECIAL INSTRUCTIONS: Spread on a sheet of waxed paper and let dry. When dry, rub the mixture between thumb and fingers to separate the lumps into fine particles. Use (sparingly) on cookies that have been iced and are still a little wet so the "pistachio" will adhere. You can also color chopped almonds in this same way.

Makes ½ cup.

DATE-NUT FILLING

INGREDIENTS	METHOD
¾ lb. (about 2 cups) pitted dried dates, cut fine ⅓ cup granulated sugar ⅓ cup water	*Combine in saucepan and cook until slightly thickened, stirring constantly. Remove from heat. Let cool.*
½ cup finely chopped nuts	*Stir in.*

SPECIAL INSTRUCTIONS: Keep any left-over portion in covered jar in refrigerator for next batch of cookies.

Makes about 2½ cups filling.

INDEX